Welsh
Words

Am restr gyflawn o lyfrau'r Lolfa, hwyliwch i mewn i'n gwefan **www.ylolfa.com** lle gallwch chwilio ac archebu ar-lein.

For a full list of Lolfa publications, go to our website **www.ylolfa.com** where you may browse and order on-line.

Steve Morris & Paul Meara

Welsh Words

Core vocabulary with phrases

Geirfa Graidd: Lefel Mynediad

yLolFa

North Wales

Argraffiad cyntaf: 2014

Cyhoeddwyd gyda chymorth ariannol
Cyngor Llyfrau Cymru

Dylunio: Robat Gruffudd/Y Lolfa

Rhif Llyfr Rhyngwladol: 978-1-84771-903-4

Cyhoeddwyd ac argraffwyd yng Nghymru
ar bapur o goedwigoedd cynaladwy gan
Y Lolfa Cyf., Talybont, Ceredigion SY24 5HE
gwefan www.ylolfa.com
e-bost ylolfa@ylolfa.com
ffôn 01970 832 304
ffacs 832 782

Diolch / Thanks

Mae'r eirfa graidd yn y llyfr hwn yn seiliedig ar brosiect ymchwil gan yr awduron ym Mhrifysgol Abertawe. Hoffem ddiolch i'r chwe deg o diwtoriaid a gyfrannodd (yn gyson, dros nifer o fisoedd) i'r ymchwil tu ôl i'r eirfa graidd. Oni bai am eich parodrwydd chi i ymgymryd â'r gwaith ychwanegol hwn, fyddai'r eirfa graidd ddim gyda ni.

Hoffem ddiolch i Mark Stonelake ac yn arbennig i Elwyn Hughes am eu sylwadau gwerthfawr ac adeiladol (yn enwedig, yn achos Elwyn, gyda/efo fersiwn y gogledd) ac i aelodau gweithgor arholiadau Mynediad a Sylfaen CBAC ac i Emyr Davies a Janette Jones, CBAC.

Ac yn olaf, diolch i Meleri Wyn James a staff y Lolfa am eu gwaith manwl a'u cyngor defnyddiol wrth fynd â'r gwaith yma i'r wasg.

The core vocabulary in this book is based on a research project by the authors at Swansea University. We would like to thank the sixty tutors who contributed (regularly, over a number of months) to the research behind this core vocabulary. Were it not for your willingness to undertake this additional work, we wouldn't have the core vocabulary.

We would like to thank Mark Stonelake and in particular Elwyn Hughes for their valuable and constructive comments (especially in Elwyn's case the north Wales version) and the members of the WJEC Mynediad and Sylfaen examinations committee and Emyr Davies and Janette Jones, at the WJEC.

And finally, thanks to Meleri Wyn James and the staff at Y Lolfa for their detailed work and their useful advice in getting this work to press.

Steve Morris & Paul Meara

HOW TO GET THE MOST OUT OF THIS BOOK

What is *Geirfa Graidd*?

The first thing to remember above all else is that this is not an exhaustive list of all the vocabulary you will ever need to be able to cope with Mynediad level Welsh for Adults! This is '**Geirfa Graidd**' – a **core vocabulary**. In other words, the items listed here are all those that our work has shown are necessary to know in order to achieve Mynediad level, that is the words you would be expected to know (and to be able to use) by the end of a Mynediad level course.

What does that mean?

It means that:

• Public Welsh for Adults exams at this level would assume you know these items and would be able to use them when you speak, write and read Welsh. Any items **not** in the **Geirfa Graidd** would normally be explained or an English translation given in brackets afterwards.

• Learning and teaching materials aimed at Mynediad level will include these items and this is the core vocabulary for inclusion in them. However, every course or learning resource will inevitably include far more items than just the **Geirfa Graidd**. The important thing to remember is that the **Geirfa Graidd: Mynediad** includes all the items you **need** to know to achieve Mynediad level, but as well as these there will be many other items of vocabulary which you will need and will be specific to you and your circumstances. Knowing these items, and being able to talk about things or people which mean a lot to you, is every bit as important as knowing the **Geirfa Graidd**: it's just that the **Geirfa Graidd** is vocabulary which is common to all learners at this level.

OK – so what's in the book?

Every item of vocabulary which forms the **Geirfa Graidd: Mynediad** is listed in this book. As well as every item of vocabulary, you will also find:

- A translation of the item into English.

- Notes to tell you if there is a more standard alternative which you might come across as well as, sometimes, whether the item causes a mutation.

- Some verbs are usually followed by certain prepositions. If this is the case, this will be also be shown. Try to remember any connections like these and memorise them together.

- When the item is a noun, you will also be given (i) the gender and (ii) the plural form, in most cases.

- In order for you to see **how** the item is used, each one includes an example of the item in context i.e. a chance for you to see it in use. These are followed by an English translation just to make the meaning and context completely clear. The examples all use patterns which should be familiar to learners towards the end of Mynediad level courses.

- Sometimes, other phrases and idioms are formed with the main item of vocabulary. These are listed under the main element e.g. *beic* [= bike] with *mynd ar gefn beic* [= to ride a bike] listed underneath it (not under 'M').

You can think of it as a mini dictionary of vocabulary which is designed specifically for adult learners of Welsh at Mynediad level. Use it to help you learn this vocabulary. To assist you further with that task, at the end of the book,

Professor Paul Meara (an international expert in vocabulary acquisition and processing), has included his top ten tips on **how** to learn vocabulary. As he says, 'you might find that the techniques don't all work for you...' and don't worry: this is normal! Every one of us learns in different ways and what works for one learner won't necessarily work for another. Experiment, and when you find a technique or techniques which help you, then concentrate on them. Some of these techniques may become more useful when you progress beyond Mynediad level, so read through them often and give them a go!

What do the abbreviations mean?

Throughout the book, we have used a few abbreviations to save space and give you more information about different items. Here's an explanation of what they mean:

[eb]	enw benywaidd	[*feminine noun*]
[eg]	enw gwrywaidd	[*masculine noun*]
[ell]	enw lluosog	[*plural noun*]

This will be helpful for you to know when it comes to actually **using** these items. For example, if you see **eb** which tells you that a noun is a *feminine noun*, you will also know that (i) it takes a soft mutation after '**y / yr / 'r**' (ii) an adjective following it will take the soft mutation and (iii) you will need the feminine versions of numbers (**dwy / tair / pedair**) instead of the masculine ones.

SW / NW	South Wales / North Wales alternatives
Treiglad Meddal	followed by a Soft Mutation
+ Treiglad Llaes	followed by an Aspirate Mutation
+ Treiglad Trwynol	followed by a Nasal Mutation

Why do some words have an asterisk * by the side of them?

A few of the items in the **Geirfa Graidd** have an asterisk by the side of them. This is to show you that they are items you should **understand** (for example, they might be items involved in classroom work e.g. **cyfieithu** – translate), but that you would not be expected to use at this level of learning Welsh.

What's not included...

Forms of verbs with endings added. The main **berfenw** (verb-noun) is included but forms with endings are not included in the list. For example, **mynd** (*to go*) is listed but **es i** (*I went*) is not. Similarly, **bod** (*to be*) is there but **roeddwn i** (*I was*) is not.

• Names of towns, cities, counties etc. This does not apply to names of countries where relevant.

• A very small number of untranslatable, pattern / grammar items.

It looks like there are some English words in the list! Why have they been included?

They might look like English words – and indeed there are many borrowings from English in Welsh. However, if they are words which are used frequently and have become accepted into contemporary spoken Welsh e.g. **pensil, lemon, ffilm**, then you need to know:

(i) that this is how to say *'pencil'*, *'lemon'* and *'film'* in Welsh

(ii) whether they are masculine or feminine (so that you know whether to use 'dau ffilm' or 'dwy ffilm' and whether you say 'ffilm da' or 'ffilm dda') and

(iii) what the plural form is.

And finally....

Mastering vocabulary appropriate to the level at which you are learning is vital to success in any language learning. Use this book to help you to learn and absorb the core vocabulary you need to succeed at Mynediad level in Welsh. Don't forget that these are the **core** words you'll need at this level. You'll also need to learn many others so that you can talk confidently at Mynediad level about everything that is important and relevant in your own particular lives. These will be specific to you and you should compile a list of them to keep handy with this book. Together they will arm you with the vocabulary you will need to reach Mynediad level and move on beyond it. Mwynhewch!

Steve Morris & Paul Meara
Swansea, July 2014

A

A / Ac   *And*
*Mi wnaeth Jack **a** Jill fynd i weld y gêm.*
*Jack **and** Jill went to see the game.*
*Mi wnaeth Siân **ac** Ifan fynd i weld y gêm.*
*Siân **and** Ifan went to see the game.*
*[Followed by **Treiglad Llaes** in formal speech]*
*Mae'r caffi'n gwerthu te **a ch**offi.*
*The café sells tea **and** coffee.*

Actor *[eg]*   *Actor*
> actorion

Actores *[eb]*   *Actress*
> actoresau
Roedd Richard Burton yn **actor** enwog.
*Richard Burton was a famous **actor.***
Roedd Elizabeth Taylor yn **actores** enwog.
*Elizabeth Taylor was a famous **actress**.*

Achos   *Because*
Mi wnes i agor y ffenest **achos** roedd hi'n boeth yn y stafell.
*I opened the window **because** it was hot in the room.*

Adeiladu   *To build*
Mi fydd Bob yn helpu i **adeiladu**'r tŷ newydd.
*Bob will help **build** the new house.*

Adeiladwr *[eg]*   *Builder*
> adeiladwyr
*Mi fydd Bob yr **adeiladwr** yn gweithio ar y tŷ newydd.*
*Bob the **builder** will be working on the new house.*

Adolygu

To revise
Cyn yr arholiad, roedd pawb yn y dosbarth yn **adolygu** efo'r tiwtor.
*Before the exam, everyone in the class was **revising** with the tutor.*

Adra

Home / Homeward > in the direction of home
Roedd yn braf mynd **adra** ar ôl y gwyliau.
*It was nice to go **home** after the holidays.*

Afal *[eg]*
> afalau

Apple
Dw i'n bwyta **afal** bob amser cinio.
*I eat an **apple** every lunch-time.*

Afon *[eb]*
> afonydd

River
Afon Hafren ac **afon** Dyfrdwy ydy dwy **afon** fawr Cymru.
*The **river** Severn and the **river** Dee are Wales' two big rivers.*

Agor

To open
Mi fydd y siop yn **agor** yfory am 08:00.
*The shop will **open** tomorrow at 08:00.*

Agos

Close, near [Standard Welsh]
Mae Stadiwm y Mileniwm yn **agos** i ganol Caerdydd.
*The Millennium Stadium is **near** the centre of Cardiff.*
*[See also: **Wrth ymyl**]*

Angen *[eg]*
> anghenion

Need
Mae **angen** help.
*There's a **need** for help > help is needed.*

Anghofio

To forget
Pwy dach chi? Dw i wedi **anghofio** eich enw chi!
*Who are you? I have **forgotten** your name!*

Allan

(i) *Out*

Rhaid i bawb fynd **allan** *o'r neuadd.*

Everyone has to go **out** of the hall.

(ii) *Exit*

Tân! Defnyddiwch y drws sy'n dweud **ALLAN**.

Fire! Use the door which says **EXIT**.

Am

About, at [+ time] + Treiglad Meddal

Mae pawb yn licio siarad **am** *y tywydd yng Nghymru.*

Everyone likes to talk **about** the weather in Wales.

Mi fydd y ddrama'n dechrau **am dd**eg o'r gloch.

The play will start **at** ten o'clock.

Ambiwlans [eg] *Ambulance*

> ambiwlansys *Mi wnaethon nhw ffonio am* **ambiwlans** *ar ôl gweld y ddamwain.*

They phoned for an **ambulance** after seeing the accident.

Amgueddfa [eb] *Museum*

> amgueddfeydd *Mae llun y* Mona Lisa *yn* **amgueddfa'r** *Louvre, Paris.*

The picture of the Mona Lisa is in the Louvre **museum**, Paris.

Amser [eg] *Time*

> amserau *Dan ni wedi mwynhau'n fawr, mae'r* **amser** *wedi hedfan.*

We've really enjoyed ourselves, the **time** has flown.

Anfon

To send > to send **to** = *anfon* **at** *[people],* **i** *[place]*

Maen nhw wedi **anfon** *y siec yn y post.*

They have **sent** the cheque in the post.

Anifail *[eg]*
> anifeiliaid

Animal
Does 'na ddim llawer o **anifeiliaid** *ar ei fferm o.*
There aren't many **animals** *on his farm.*

Anifail anwes

Pet
Mae llawer o bobl yn cadw ci fel **anifail anwes**.
Lots of people keep a dog as a **pet**.

Anifail gwyllt

Wild animal
Roedd y plentyn yn rhedeg o gwmpas fel **anifail gwyllt**.
The child was running about like a **wild animal**.

Annwyd *[eg]*

[a] Cold
Dw i ddim yn teimlo'n dda – mae gen i annwyd.
I don't feel well – I've got a **cold.**

Annwyl

(i) Cute
Mae'r gath fach yna'n **annwyl** *iawn.*
That little cat's very **cute.**
(ii) Dear
Annwyl *syr /* **Annwyl** *fadam…*
Dear *sir /* **Dear** *madam…*

Anodd

Difficult
Dydy'r treigladau yn Gymraeg ddim yn **anodd** *iawn.*
The mutations in Welsh aren't very **difficult.**

Anrheg *[eb]*
> anrhegion

Present, gift
Ar ei ben-blwydd mi wnaeth hi gael llawer o **anrhegion** *hyfryd.*
On her birthday she had many wonderful **presents.**

Ar

On + Treiglad Meddal
Wnest ti weld y rhaglen **ar** *y teledu neithiwr?*

Did you see the programme **on** *the television last night?*

Mae'r bwyd yn barod – mae o **ar** *y bwrdd.*
The food's ready – it's **on** *the table.*

Pawb allan! Mae'r tŷ **ar** *dân!*
Everybody out! The house is **on** *fire!*

Ar agor	*Open*
	Mae'r siop **ar agor** *trwy'r dydd.*
	The shop is **open** *all day.*
Ar ben	*Over, finished, at the end of*
	Rwyt ti'n byw **ar ben** *arall y ffordd i mi.*
	You live **at** *the other* **end of** *the road to me.*
	Does 'na neb yma rŵan – mae popeth **ar ben**.
	There's nobody here now – everything's **over / finished**.
Ar eich traed!	*On your feet! Stand up!*
Ar gael	*Available*
	Mi fydd coffi **ar gael** *cyn y cyfarfod.*
	Coffee will be **available** *before the meeting.*
	Pwy sy **ar gael** *i weithio heno?*
	Who's **available** *to work tonight?*
Ar gau	*Closed*
	Fel arfer, mae'r siop **ar gau** *ar ddydd Sul.*
	Usually, the shop is **closed** *on Sunday.*
Ar hyn o bryd	*At the moment*
	Ar hyn o bryd *does 'na neb yma.*
	At the moment *there's nobody here.*
Ar ôl	*(i) After*
	Lle dach chi'n mynd **ar ôl** *y gêm?*
	Where are you going **after** *the game?*
	(ii) Left, remaining
	Mae pawb wedi bwyta'n dda – does 'na ddim bwyd **ar ôl**.
	Everyone has eaten well – there's no food **left**.

Araf
Slow
*Rhaid i chi yrru'n **araf** yma.*
*You must drive **slowly** here.*

Arall
Other
> eraill
*Oes 'na rywun **arall** yn dŵad i'r dosbarth heno?*
*Is there anyone else – (lit: anyone **other**) – coming to class tonight?*
*Oes, mae 'na bobl **eraill** yn dŵad i'r dosbarth heno.*
*Yes, there are **other** people coming to class tonight.*

Ardderchog
Excellent
*Yn ôl y tiwtor, mae gwaith y dysgwyr yn **ardderchog** – maen nhw'n siarad yn dda iawn.*
*According to the tutor, the learners' work is **excellent** – they speak very well.*

Arholiad *[eg]*
Exam
> arholiadau
*Mae pawb yn mynd i wneud **arholiad** yn yr haf.*
*Everyone's going to do an **exam** in the summer.*

Arian *[eg]*
Money [Standard Welsh]
See > **Pres**

Aros
(i) To wait > (to wait **for** = aros **am**)
*Roedd 'na lawer o bobl yn **aros** am y bws i fynd i'r dre.*
*Many people were **waiting** for the bus to go to town.*
(ii) To stay
*Dan ni'n mynd i **aros** mewn gwesty ar ein gwyliau.*
*We are going to **stay** in a hotel on our holidays.*

At
To [a person] + *Treiglad Meddal*
Mi wnes i ysgrifennu llythyr **at** *fy modryb i ddiolch am yr anrheg.*
I wrote a letter **to** *my auntie to say thank you for the present.*
Mi wnes i anfon y siec **at f**ab fy chwaer.
I sent the cheque **to** *my sister's son.*

Ateb *[eg]*
> atebion
An answer, a reply
Dw i ddim wedi cael **ateb** *i'r cwestiwn eto.*
I haven't had a **reply** *to the question yet.*

Ateb *[verb]*
To answer, to reply
Mi wnes i **ateb** *dy lythyr y bore yma.*
I **answer**ed *your letter this morning.*

Athro *[eg]*
> athrawon
Teacher [male]

Athrawes *[eb]*
> athrawesau
Teacher [female]
Mae Mr Evans yn gweithio fel **athro** *Cymraeg.*
Mr Evans works as a Welsh **(male) teacher**.
Mae Mrs Jenkins yn gweithio fel **athrawes** *Saesneg.*
Mrs Jenkins works as an English **(female) teacher**.

Awr *[eb]*
> oriau
Hour
Mi wnaethon ni gyrraedd yma dros **awr** *yn ôl ond dan ni ddim wedi gweld neb eto.*
We arrived here over an **hour** *ago but we haven't seen anyone yet.*

Awst *[mis]*
August
Fel arfer, dan ni'n licio mynd i'r Eisteddfod ym mis **Awst**.
Usually, we like to go to the Eisteddfod in **August**.

B

Baban *[eg]*   *Baby [See also:* **Babi***]*
> babanod   *Ydy'r* **baban** *yn cysgu eto?*
Babi *[eg]*   *Is the* **baby** *sleeping yet?*
> babis

Bacwn *[eg]*   *Bacon*
   Mi wnaethon ni fwyta wy, **bacwn** *a sglodion
i ginio.*
   We ate egg, **bacon** *and chips for lunch.*

Bach   *Small, little*
   Enw fy mrawd **bach** *ydy Ifan.*
   The name of my **little** *brother is Ifan.*

Bachgen *[eg]*   *Boy [Standard Welsh]*
> bechgyn   *See >* **Hogyn / hogiau**

Bag *[eg]*   *Bag*
> bagiau   *Pris* **bag** *siopa yng Nghymru ydy pum ceiniog.*
   The price of a shopping **bag** *in Wales is five
pence.*

Banc *[eg]*   *Bank*
> banciau   *Rhaid i mi alw yn y* **banc** *i gael pres.*
   I have to call in the **bank** *to get money.*

Bara *[eg]*   *Bread*
   Mae **bara** *brown yn dda i chi.*
   Brown **bread** *is good for you.*

Bara menyn   *Bread and butter (also as an idiom)*
   O na! Dim **bara menyn** *i de eto!*
   Oh no! Not **bread and butter** *for tea again!*
   Mae hi'n ennill ei **bara menyn** *yn gweithio mewn siop.*
   She earns her **bread and butter** *working in a shop.*

Bara brith   *No English translation. (lit: speckled bread. It's a kind
of rich fruit loaf).*

Bara lawr   *Laver bread*
*Mae marchnad Abertawe'n enwog am ei **bara lawr**.*
*Swansea market is famous for its **laver bread**.*

Bath *[eg]*   *Bath*
*Doedd y plant ddim yn licio amser **bath**.*
The children didn't like **bath time.**

Be'?   **What?** *[Standard Welsh: **Beth?**]*
Beic *[eg]*   *Bike*
> beiciau   *Mae defnyddio **beic** yn dda i'r iechyd.*
Using a **bike is good for the health.**

Mynd ar gefn beic   *To ride a bike*
*Mi wnaethon ni **fynd ar gefn beic** i lawr i'r parc.*
We **rode a bike down to the park.**

Beiro *[eg/eb]*   *Biro*
> beiros   *Does 'na ddim llawer o **feiro** coch ar fy
ngwaith cartre!*
There's not much red **biro on my homework!**

Bendigedig   *Wonderful*
*Mi wnaethon ni gael parti **bendigedig** ar ei
phen-blwydd yn 25 oed.*
We had a **wonderful party on her 25th
birthday.**

Benthyg   *To loan / Lend*
> rhoi benthyg i   *Wnei di **roi benthyg** £50 i ni?*
Will you **loan / lend us £50?**

Cael benthyg   *To borrow*
*Dach chi wedi **cael benthyg** £100 gen i'n barod!*
You've already **borrowed £100 from me!**

Benywaidd*   *Feminine > Enw benywaidd = Feminine noun*
Beth?   **What?** *[Standard Welsh]*
*See > **Be'?***

Bisgedi	*Biscuits [ell]*
bisgeden *[eb]*	*Dach chi'n licio **bisgedi** efo'ch te?*
	*Do you like **biscuits** with your tea?*
Ble?	*Where? [Standard Welsh]*
	See > **Lle?**
Blino	*To tire > wedi blino = tired*
	*Mi wnaethon ni weithio'n galed yn y dosbarth heno. Mae pawb **wedi blino**.*
	*We worked hard in class tonight. Everyone is **tired**.*
Blwyddyn *[eb]*	*Year*
> blynyddoedd	*Dan ni'n edrych ymlaen at ddŵad yn ôl y **flwyddyn** nesa.*
	*We're looking forward to coming back next **year**.*
Bod	*To be*
	*Mae'n bwysig **bod** yn y neuadd erbyn saith o'r gloch.*
	*It's important **to be** in the hall by seven o'clock.*
Bol *[eg]*	*Stomach, belly*
> boliau	*Dw i wedi bwyta gormod. Mae fy **mol** i'n llawn...*
	*I've eaten too much. My **stomach** is full...*
Poen bol	*Stomach ache*
	*... ond sgen i ddim **poen bol**!*
	*... but I haven't got **stomach ache**!*
Bore *[eg]*	*Morning*
> boreau	*Mi fydd hi'n bwrw glaw yn y **bore** ond mi fydd hi'n sych yn y prynhawn.*
	*It will be raining in the **morning** but it will be dry in the afternoon.*

Braf

Fine [doesn't mutate]
Roedd y tywydd yn **braf** *pan wnaethon ni fynd i Sbaen.*
The weather was **fine** *when we went to Spain.*

Braich *[eb]*
> breichiau

Arm
Mi wnaeth Elin dorri ei **braich** *yn y ddamwain.*
Elin broke her **arm** *in the accident.*

Brawd *[eg]*
> brodyr

Brother
Mae gen i un **brawd** *ac mae o'n byw yn Wrecsam.*
I have one **brother** *and he lives in Wrexham.*

Brawd yng nghyfraith *Brother-in-law*

Enw fy **mrawd yng nghyfraith** *(brawd fy ngwraig) ydy Ifor.*
My **brother-in-law** *(my wife's brother)'s name is Ifor.*

Brawddeg* *[eb] Sentence*
> brawddegau*

Brecwast *[eg]*

Breakfast
Dw i'n licio bwyta **brecwast** *yn y gwely bob dydd Sul.*
I like to eat **breakfast** *in bed every Sunday.*

Brechdan *[eb]*
> brechdanau

Sandwich
Dan ni'n mwynhau **brechdan** *ham a chaws i ginio.*
We enjoy a ham and cheese **sandwich** *for lunch.*

Bron (yn)

Almost
Mae'n hwyr iawn – mae hi **bron yn** *un o'r gloch yn y bore.*
It's very late – it's **almost** *one o'clock in the morning.*

Brown

Brown
Mae gwallt hir, **brown** *gan fy mam.*
My mother has got long, **brown** *hair.*

Brws(h) *[eg]*   *Brush*
> brwshys   *Maen nhw'n defnyddio eu **brwsh** dannedd*
                       bob tro.
                       *They use their tooth**brush** every time*

Brwsio   *To brush*
                       *Mae'r plant yn **brwsio** eu dannedd bob nos.*
                       *The children **brush** their teeth every night.*

Bwrdd *[eg]*   *Table*
> byrddau   *Dowch i eistedd wrth y **bwrdd** – mae bwyd*
                       yn barod.
                       *Come and sit at the **table** – food is ready.*

Bwrw glaw /   *To rain / snow*
eira   *Yn y bore, mi fydd hi'n **bwrw eira** yn y*
                       *mynyddoedd ond mi fydd hi'n **bwrw glaw***
                       erbyn y prynhawn.
                       *In the morning, it will be **snowing** in the*
                       mountains but by the afternoon it will be
                       ***raining**.*

Bws *[eg]*   *Bus*
> bysiau   *Mae'r **bws** yn mynd o ganol y dre i lawr i'r*
                       môr.
                       *The **bus** goes from the town centre down to*
                       the sea.

Bwyd *[eg]*   *Food*
> bwydydd   *Rhaid i ni fynd i'r siop – does 'na ddim*
                       ***bwyd** ar ôl.*
                       *We have to go to the shop – there's no **food***
                       left.

Bwydo   *To feed*
                       *Mae'r ffermwr yn **bwydo** ei anifeiliaid.*
                       *The farmer is **feeding** his animals.*

Bwydlen *[eb]*   *Menu*
> bwydlenni   *Dw i ddim yn gwybod be' i fwyta – dw i'n
mynd i edrych ar y **fwydlen**.*
*I don't know what to eat – I'm going to look
at the **menu**.*

Bwyta   *To eat*
*Fel arfer, dan ni'n **bwyta** am saith o'r gloch.*
*Usually, we **eat** at seven o'clock.*

Bwyta allan   *To eat out*
*Maen nhw'n **bwyta allan** unwaith yr wythnos.*
*They **eat out** once a week.*

Tŷ bwyta   *Restaurant*
*Maen nhw'n gwneud bwyd da yn y **tŷ bwyta** newydd.*
*They do good food in the new **restaurant**.*

Byr   *Short*
*Mae'n anodd rhoi ateb **byr** i'r cwestiwn.*
*It's difficult to give a **short** answer to the
question.*

Bys *[eg]*   *Finger*
> bysedd   *Yn y ddamwain, mi wnaeth hi golli ei **bys**.*
*In the accident, she lost her **finger**.*

Byth   *Ever / Never*
*Dw i **byth** isio gweld y ffilm yna eto.*
*I **never** want to see that film again.*

*Cymru am **byth**!*   *Wales for **ever**!*

Byw   *To live*
*Dach chi wedi symud tŷ? Lle dach chi'n **byw**
rŵan?*
*Have you moved house? Where do you **live**
now?*

C

Cacen *[eb]*
> cacennau

Cake

*Mi wnaethon ni brynu **cacen** siocled fawr ar ei pen-blwydd hi.*

*We bought a big chocolate **cake** on her birthday.*

*[See also: **Teisen**]*

Cadair *[eb]*
> cadeiriau

Chair

*Roedd 'na fwrdd a phedair **cadair** yn y stafell fwyta.*

*There was a table and four **chairs** in the dining room.*

Cadw

To keep

*Dydyn nhw ddim yn **cadw** eu car yn y garej.*

*They don't **keep** their car in the garage.*

Cadw'n heini

To keep fit

*Mae 'na ddosbarth **cadw'n heini** yn y ganolfan chwaraeon.*

*There's a **keep fit** class in the sports centre.*

Cael

To have, to get

*Dw i'n **cael** brecwast am saith o'r gloch fel arfer...*

*Usually I **have** breakfast at seven o'clock...*

*... ond ddoe mi wnes i **gael** brecwast am wyth o'r gloch.*

*... but yesterday I **had** breakfast at eight o'clock.*

Caffi *[eg]*

Café

*Maen nhw'n gwerthu coffi hyfryd yn y **caffi** yma.*

*They sell lovely coffee in this **café**.*

Camera *[eg]* *Camera*
> camerâu *Wyt ti'n gwybod sut mae'r* **camera** *newydd yn gweithio?*
Do you know how the new **camera** *works?*

Canol *[eg]* *Centre, middle*
Dydy **canol** *y dre ddim yn fawr iawn.*
The centre *of the town / town* **centre** *isn't very big.*

Yng nghanol *In the middle, centre of*
Maen nhw'n adeiladu fflatiau newydd **yng nghanol** *y dre.*
They're building new flats **in the middle / centre** *of town / in the town* **centre.**

Canolfan *[eb]* *Centre [i.e. leisure, shopping, sports centre]*
> canolfannau

Canolfan chwaraeon *Sports centre*
Dan ni'n chwarae hoci yn y **ganolfan chwaraeon.**
We play hockey in the **sports centre.**

Canolfan hamdden *Leisure centre*
Mi wnaeth y plant fynd i'r **ganolfan hamdden** *i nofio.*
The children went to the **leisure centre** *to swim.*

Canolfan siopa *Shopping centre*
Roedd 'na lawer o bobl yn y **ganolfan siopa** *cyn y Nadolig.*
There were lots of people in the **shopping centre** *before Christmas.*

Canu *(i) To sing*
Mae côr Aberheli'n **canu** *yn Gymraeg.*
Aberheli choir **sing** *in Welsh.*

(ii) To ring [phone]
*Mae'r ffôn yn **canu**. Atebwch o!*
The phone's **ringing**. Answer it!

Capel *[eg]*
> capeli

Chapel
*Mi fydd y cyngerdd Nadolig yn y **capel** heno.*
The Christmas concert will be in the **chapel** tonight.

Car *[eg]*
> ceir

Car
*Dach chi'n medru gadael y **car** yn y maes parcio.*
You can leave the **car** in the car park.

Carafán *[eb]*
> carafanau

Caravan
*Mi wnaethon ni aros mewn **carafán** yr haf yma.*
We stayed in a **caravan** this summer.

Cardigan *[eb]*
> cardiganau

Cardigan
*Yn y gaea, dw i'n gwisgo **cardigan** bob dydd.*
In the winter, I wear a **cardigan** every day.

Cariad *[eg]*
> cariadon

(i) Boyfriend / Girlfriend / Lover
*Mae **cariad** Siân yn dŵad o'r Eidal.*
Siân's **boyfriend** comes from Italy.
*Mae **cariad** Ffred yn dŵad o'r Alban.*
Ffred's **girlfriend** comes from Scotland.
(ii) Love [noun]
*Pen-blwydd hapus! Llawer o **gariad**, Mam a Dad.*
Happy birthday! Lots of **love**, Mam and Dad.

Cartre *[eg]*
> cartrefi

Home
*Pob hwyl i chi yn eich **cartre** newydd!*
All the best to you in your new **home**!
*Enw'r **cartre** hen bobl ydy Bryn Awelon.*
The name of the old people's **home** is Bryn Awelon.

Caru
To love
*Dw i'n dy **garu** di.*
I **love** you.

Castell *[eg]*
> cestyll
Castle
*Dach chi wedi gweld y **castell** yng Nghaernarfon?*
*Have you seen the **castle** in Caernarfon?*

Cath *[eb]*
> cathod
Cat
*Mae ein **cath** ni'n licio yfed llefrith a chysgu.*
*Our **cat** likes to drink milk and sleep.*

Cau
To shut, close
*Mae'r siop yn **cau** am bump o'r gloch.*
*The shop **shuts** at five o'clock.*

Caws *[eg]*
Cheese
***Caws** gwyn ydy caws Caerffili.*
*Caerphilly **cheese** is white **cheese**.*

Cefn *[eg]*
> cefnau
Back [of the body or of a place]
*Mi wnaethon ni eistedd yn y **cefn**.*
*We sat at the **back**.*

Poen cefn
Backache
*Dw i ddim yn gweithio – mae gen i **boen cefn**.*
*I'm not working – I've got **backache**.*

Ceg *[eb]*
> cegau
Mouth
*Mae'r deintydd yn deud: 'Agorwch eich **ceg**!'*
*The dentist says: 'Open your **mouth**!'*

Cegin *[eb]*
> ceginau
Kitchen
*Mae 'na **gegin** fawr yn y tŷ newydd.*
*There's a big **kitchen** in the new house.*

Ceiniog *[eb]*
> ceiniogau
Penny / Pence
*Pris y papur ydy pum deg **ceiniog**.*
*The price of the paper is fifty **pence**.*

Cerdyn post *[eg]* *Postcard*

> cardiau post *Pob hwyl ar y gwyliau! Cofiwch anfon* **cerdyn post***.*
All the best for the holidays! Remember to send a **postcard***.*

Cerdded *To walk*
Rhaid i'r plant **gerdded** *i'r ysgol.*
The children must **walk** *to school.*

Ci *[eg]* *Dog*
> cŵn *Dw i'n mynd â'r* **ci** *am dro bob dydd.*
I take the **dog** *for a walk every day.*

Cig *[eg]* *Meat*
> cigoedd *Mi wnes i fwyta'r* **cig** *ond dim y llysiau.*
I ate the **meat** *but not the vegetables.*

Cig eidion *Beef*

Cig moch *Bacon [bacwn] or pork [porc]*

Cig oen *Lamb*

Cinio *[eg]* *Lunch / Dinner*
> ciniawau *Mi fyddwn ni'n bwyta* **cinio** *am un o'r gloch heddiw.*
We will be eating **dinner** *at one o'clock today.*

Cloc *[eg]* *(i) Clock*
> clociau *Mae'r* **cloc** *ar y wal yn araf.*
The **clock** *on the wall is slow.*
(ii) O'clock = O'r gloch
Mae'n wyth **o'r gloch** *– amser brecwast.*
It's eight **o'clock** *– time for breakfast.*

Clust *[eb/eg]* *Ear*
> clustiau *Gair yn eich* **clust***, os gwelwch yn dda.*
A word in your **ear***, please.*

Pigyn clust

Earache / A bad ear
Dw i ddim yn clywed yn dda – mae gen i
bigyn clust.
I don't hear well – I've got **earache / a bad ear**.

Clwb *[eg]*
> clybiau

Club
Mae **clwb** *pêl-droed Abertawe'n chwarae yn y Liberty.*
Swansea football **club** *play at the Liberty.*

Clwb nos

Night club
Mi fydd y **clwb nos** *ar agor tan ddau o'r gloch y bore.*
The **night club** *will be open until two o'clock in the morning.*

Clywed

To hear
Mae'n anodd **clywed** *y tiwtor yng nghefn y stafell.*
It's difficult / hard to **hear** *the tutor at the back of the room.*

Coch

Red
Mi wnes i yfed gormod o win **coch** *neithiwr.*
I drank too much **red** *wine last night.*

Codi

(i) to get up
Faint o'r gloch dach chi'n **codi** *yn y bore?*
What time do you **get up** *in the morning?*
(ii) to pick / lift up / to raise
Mae'n anodd **codi**'*r ci – mae o'n fawr.*
It's difficult to **pick up** *the dog – he's big.*
(iii) to go up
Mae pris petrol wedi **codi**.
The price of petrol has **gone up**.

Coes *[eb]*
> coesau

Leg
Mi wnaeth Eleri dorri ei **choes** *ar y mynydd.*
Eleri broke her **leg** *on the mountain.*

Cofio

To remember
*Dw i ddim yn medru **cofio** ei enw o.*
I can't remember his **name**.

Coffi [eg]

Coffee
*Dw i'n yfed **coffi** mawr bob bore.*
I drink a large **coffee** every morning.

Coginio

To cook
*Mae fy ffrind i'n **coginio** pasta bob nos.*
My friend **cooks** pasta every night.

Coleg [eg]
> colegau

College
*Ar ôl gadael yr ysgol, mae hi isio mynd i'r **coleg**.*
After leaving school, she wants to go to **college**

Colli

To lose
*Mi wnaeth Cymru **golli** 2–1 yn erbyn Ffrainc.*
Wales **lost** 2–1 against France.

Côr [eg]
> corau

Choir
*Mi wnaeth y **côr** ganu i godi pres i'r eisteddfod.*
The **choir** sang to raise money for the eisteddfod.

Côt [eb]
> cotiau

Coat
*Mi fydd hi'n gwisgo **côt** trwy'r gaea.*
She will be wearing a **coat** throughout the winter.

Côt law

Raincoat
*Mae hi'n bwrw glaw: dw i'n mynd i wisgo **côt law**.*
It's raining: I'm going to wear a **raincoat**.

Credu

To believe, to think
*Dw i ddim yn **credu** eu stori nhw o gwbl.*
I don't **believe** their story at all.

Cur pen

Headache
*Roedd y canu'n ofnadwy – roedd gen i **gur pen**!*
The singing was awful – I had a **headache**!

Cwestiwn *[eg]*   *Question*
> cwestiynau   *Doedd y tiwtor ddim yn medru ateb y*
    cwestiwn.
    The tutor couldn't answer the **question**.

Cwrs *[eg]*   *Course*
> cyrsiau   *Roedd y* **cwrs** *yn dda iawn. Mi wnaethon ni*
    ddysgu llawer o eiriau newydd.
    The **course** *was very good. We learnt lots of*
    new words.

Cwrw *[eg]*   *Beer*
    Mae'r dafarn yn gwerthu **cwrw** *o Gymru.*
    The pub sells **beer** *from Wales.*

Cychwyn   *To start*
    Mae'r daith yn **cychwyn** *yn Wrecsam.*
    The trip **starts** *in Wrexham.*

Cyfan*   *All, everything*

Cyfarfod *[eg]*   *A meeting*
> cyfarfodydd   *Mi fydd y* **cyfarfod** *yn neuadd y dre.*
    The **meeting** *will be in the town hall.*

Cyfarfod *[verb]*   *To meet*
    Dan ni'n **cyfarfod** *Siân yn y maes parcio.*
    We're **meeting** *Siân in the car park.*

Cyfeiriad *[eg]*   *Address*
> cyfeiriadau   *Dan ni wedi symud tŷ. Dach chi isio'r*
    cyfeiriad *newydd?*
    We have moved house. Do you want the new
    address?

Cyfieithu*   *To translate* > **Cyfieithwch!** = *Translate!*

Cyflym   *Quick / Quickly*
    Mi wnaeth y ci redeg yn **gyflym** *iawn.*
    The dog ran very **quickly**.

Cyfrifiadur *[eg] Computer*

> cyfrifiaduron   *Dydy'r* **cyfrifiadur** *ddim yn gweithio. Dan ni wedi colli popeth!*

The **computer** *isn't working. We've lost everything!*

Cyngerdd *[eg/eb] Concert*

> cyngherddau   *Mi wnaeth Katherine Jenkins ganu yn y* **cyngerdd** *mawr yng Nghaerdydd.*

Katherine Jenkins sang in the big **concert** *in Cardiff.*

Cymraeg   *(i) Welsh language [adjective]*

Rhaglen **Gymraeg** *ydy Pobol y Cwm.*

Pobol y Cwm *is a* **Welsh (language)** *programme.*

(i) Welsh language [noun]

Oes 'na rywun yn siarad **Cymraeg** *yn y swyddfa?*

Does anyone speak **Welsh** *in the office?*

Cymro *[eg]*   *A Welshman*

Cymraes *[eb]*   *A Welsh woman*

> Cymry   *The Welsh*

Cymro *ydy Ifan – mae o'n dŵad o Fangor yn wreiddiol.*

Ifan is **Welsh** *(i.e. a Welshman) – he comes from Bangor originally.*

Cymraes *ydy Eleri – mae hi'n dŵad o Bontypridd yn wreiddiol.*

Eleri is **Welsh** *(i.e. a Welsh woman) – she comes from Pontypridd originally.*

Cymru *[eb]*   *Wales*

Mi fydd y rhaglen ar BBC **Cymru** *heno.*

The programme will be on BBC **Wales** *tonight.*

Cymryd
To take [i.e. to receive, accept]
Dach chi'n **cymryd** *siwgr a llefrith yn eich coffi?*
Do you **take** *sugar and milk in your coffee?*

Cymylog
Cloudy
Mae'n **gymylog** *iawn heddiw ond dydy hi ddim yn bwrw glaw eto.*
It's very **cloudy** *today but it isn't raining yet.*

Cyn
Before
Mi fydd pawb yn cyrraedd **cyn** *deg o'r gloch.*
Everyone will arrive **before** *ten o'clock.*

Cyn bo hir
Soon, before long
Maen nhw wedi gadael y tŷ ond mi fyddan nhw'n ôl **cyn bo hir**.
They've left the house but they will be back **soon**.

Cynnar
Early
Mi wnaeth y trên adael yn hwyr ond mi wnaethon ni gyrraedd yn **gynnar**.
The train left late but we arrived **early**.

Cyrraedd
To arrive [at/in]
Mi fyddwn ni'n **cyrraedd** *Sbaen yn y prynhawn.*
We'll be **arriving** *in Spain in the afternoon.*

Cyrri *[eg]*
> cyrïau
Curry
Mae'r **cyrri***, Vindaloo, yn boeth iawn.*
The **curry***, Vindaloo, is very hot.*

Cysgu
To sleep
Mi wnaeth y baban fynd i **gysgu***'n syth ar ôl bwyd.*
The baby went to **sleep** *straight away after food.*

Cyw iâr *[eg]*
> cywion ieir
Chicken
Maen nhw'n cael **cyw iâr** *a sglodion i swper.*
They're having **chicken** *and chips for supper.*

CH

Chi

(i) You [formal singular]
*Bore da, Mrs Jones. Sut dach **chi** heddiw?*
Good morning, Mrs Jones. How are you today?
(ii) You [formal and informal plural]
*Siwan a Lowri, dach **chi**'n barod?*
Siwan and Lowri, are you ready?
(iii) Your [formal singular and plural] (+ eich)
*Ydy eich plant **chi**'n mynd i ysgol Gymraeg?*
Do your children go to a Welsh (language) school?

Chwaer *[eb]*
> chwiorydd

Sister
*Mae gen i ddwy **chwaer** ac maen nhw'n byw yn y Rhondda.*
I have two sisters and they live in the Rhondda.

Chwaer yng nghyfraith *Sister-in-law*

*Enw fy **chwaer yng nghyfraith** (chwaer fy ngwraig) ydy Mair.*
My sister-in-law (my wife's sister)'s name is Mair.

Chwarae

To play
*Roedd y plant yn mwynhau **chwarae** efo eu teganau.*
The children were enjoying playing with their toys.

Chwaraeon *[ell]* *Sports, games*
*Maen nhw'n dysgu llawer o **chwaraeon** yn yr ysgol.*
They learn lots of sports in school.

Chwarter *[eg]*   *Quarter*
*Mi fydd pawb yma mewn **chwarter** awr.*
Everyone will be here in a **quarter** of an hour.

Chwefror *[mis]*   *February*
*Mis rhif dau ydy mis **Chwefror**.*
***February** is month number two.*

Chwith   *Left*
*Trowch i'r **chwith** ar ôl yr ysgol...*
Turn to the **left** after the school...
*... ac mae ein tŷ ni ar y **chwith**.*
*... and our house is on the **left**.*

D

Da   *Good / Well*
*Mae côr Aberheli yn gôr **da**...*
Côr Aberheli is a **good** choir...
*... maen nhw'n canu'n **dda**.*
*... they sing **well**.*

Dallt   *To understand [Standard Welsh: **Deall**]*
*Dw i ddim yn eich **dallt** chi. Dach chi'n siarad yn rhy gyflym.*
I don't **understand** you. You're speaking too fast.

Damwain *[eb]*   *Accident*
> damweiniau   *Mi wnaeth y **ddamwain** ddigwydd am ddeg o'r gloch neithiwr.*
The **accident** happened at ten o'clock last night.

Dan   *Under + Treiglad Meddal*
*Roedd y ci'n chwarae **dan** y bwrdd.*
The dog was playing **under** the table.
*Mi wnaeth y ci fynd **dan g**ar fy mrawd.*
The dog went **under** my brother's car.

Dangos
To show >to show someone something =
*dangos rhywbeth **i** rywun*
*Mi fydd S4C yn **dangos** y ffilm am Richard Burton fory.*
*S4C will **show** the film about Richard Burton tomorrow.*

Dant *[eg]*
> dannedd
Tooth
*Dan ni'n glanhau ein **dannedd** bob nos.*
*We clean our **teeth** every night.*

Darllen
`
To read
*Dw i'n **darllen** y papur bob dydd.*
*I **read** the paper every day.*

Darllen **am**
*To read **about***
*Mi wnes i **ddarllen am** y ddamwain yn y papur.*
*I **read about** the accident in the paper.*

Dawns *[eb]*
> dawnsfeydd
Dance
*Mi fydd 'na **ddawns** fawr yn neuadd y pentre heno.*
*There will be a big **dance** in the village hall tonight.*

Dawnsio
To dance
*Rwyt ti'n mynd i **ddawnsio** yn y sioe.*
*You're going to **dance** in the show.*

De *[eg]*
South
*Mae Mam yn dod o'r **de** yn wreiddiol.*
*My mother comes from the **south** originally.*

De *[eb]*
Right [i.e. opposite to 'left']
*Trowch i'r **dde** ar ôl y capel...*
*Turn to the **right** after the chapel...*
*... ac mae ein tŷ ni ar y **dde**.*
*... and out house is on the **right**.*

Deall
To understand [Standard Welsh]
*See > **Dallt***

Dechrau
To begin
Pryd mae'r cyngerdd yn **dechrau***?*
When does the concert **begin***?*

Defnyddio
To use
Dan ni ddim yn medru **defnyddio***'r peiriant golchi newydd.*
We can't **use** **the new washing machine.**

Deffro
To wake up
Dydy Alun ddim wedi **deffro** *eto: mae o'n cysgu yn y gwely.*
Alun hasn't **woken up** **yet: he's sleeping in bed.**

Deialog *[eb]* *
Dialogue

Deintydd *[eg]*
Dentist
> deintyddion
Mi fydd y **deintydd** *yn edrych ar fy nannedd y prynhawn yma.*
The **dentist** **will be looking at my teeth this afternoon.**

Del
Pretty, cute
Mae gynnyn nhw faban bach **del***.*
They've got a **pretty / cute** **little baby.**
Roedd yr hogan yn edrych yn **ddel** *yn ei het newydd.*
The girl looked **pretty** **in her new hat.**

Deud
To say [Standard Welsh: **Dweud***]*
Sut dach chi'n **deud** *X yn Gymraeg?*
How do you **say** *X* **in Welsh?**

Deud wrth
To tell [Standard Welsh: **Dweud wrth***]*
Dwyt ti ddim wedi **deud** *popeth* **wrth** *yr heddlu.*
You haven't **told** **the police everything.**

Diddordeb *[eg]*
Interest
> diddordebau
Be' ydy eich **diddordebau** *chi?*
What are your **interests***?*

Diflas	*Miserable [can also mean 'boring' e.g. see >* **Drama]**
	Roedd hi'n **ddiflas** *ddoe, yn bwrw glaw trwy'r dydd.*
	It was **miserable** *yesterday, raining all day.*
Digon [o]	*Enough*
	Dach chi wedi cael **digon** *o fwyd? Dach chi wedi cael* **digon***?*
	Have you had **enough** *food? Have you had* **enough***?*
Digwydd	*To happen*
	Beth sy'n **digwydd** *yn y dre heno?*
	What's **happening** *in town tonight?*
Dillad [ell]	*Clothes*
	Roedd Nain yn golchi'r **dillad** *bob dydd Llun.*
	My gran used to wash the **clothes** *every Monday.*
Dillad chwaraeon	*Sportswear / clothes*
	Mi fyddwn ni'n gwisgo **dillad chwaraeon** *yn y dosbarth cadw'n heini heno.*
	We will be wearing **sportswear** *in the keep fit class tonight.*
Dillad nofio	*Swimwear*
	Mi wnaeth hi wisgo ei **dillad nofio** *yn y pwll nofio.*
	She wore her **swimwear** *in the swimming pool.*
Dillad nos	*Nightwear*
	Dan ni'n gwisgo **dillad nos** *yn y gwely.*
	We wear **nightwear** *in bed.*
Dim / Ddim	*Used to make the negative*
	Does gen i **ddim** *pres.*
	I have **not** */ I have***n't** *got any money.*
Dim	*No / Not (+ a noun)*

Dim *Saesneg yn y dosbarth –* **dim** *un gair o Saesneg!*
No *English in class –* **not** *one word of English!*
Popeth yn iawn, dim problem o gwbl.
Everything's fine, no problem at all.

Dim ond	*Only*
	Faint o bobl oedd yn y dosbarth? **Dim ond** *Rhys a fi.*
	How many people were in class? **Only** *Rhys and me.*
Dim (byd)	*Nothing / Anything*
	Wnes i ddim deud dim byd.
	I said nothing / I didn't say anything.
Diod *[eb]* > diodydd	*Drink [noun]*
	Mi fydd 'na fwyd a diod yn y parti.
	There will be food and drink in the party.
	Dw i'n licio cael diod efo fy mwyd.
	I like to have a drink with my food.
Diolch (i)	*Thank you*
	Dw i'n licio'r anrheg. Diolch yn fawr i chi!
	I like the present. Thank you very much / Many thanks to you!
Dis *[eg]*	*Dice*
	Pwy sy'n mynd nesa? Mae'r dis gen i.
	Who goes next? I've got the dice!
Di-waith	*Unemployed, out of work*
	Dydy o ddim yn gweithio rŵan. Mae o'n ddi-waith.
	He's not working now. He's unemployed / out of work.
Diwedd *[eg]*	*End, finish*
	Roedd diwedd y ffilm yn drist.
	The end of the film was sad.
Diwetha	*Last [i.e. most recent]*
	Mi wnaeth y llythyr ddŵad ddydd Llun diwetha.
	The letter came last Monday.

Diwrnod *[eg]*   *Day*
Dw i ddim yn cofio'r **diwrnod** *cynta yn yr ysgol.*
I don't remember the first day at school.
Dim gwaith fory! Mae gen i **ddiwrnod** *o wyliau.*
No work tomorrow! I've got a day off.

Dod   *To come [Standard Welsh]*
See > **Dŵad**

Dod â   *To bring [Standard Welsh]*
See > **Dŵad â**

Doli *[eb]*   *Dolly*
> doliau   *Roedd Megan isio cael* **doli** *newydd y Nadolig yma.*
Megan wanted to have a new dolly this Christmas.

Dosbarth *[eg]*   *Class*
> dosbarthiadau   *Dan ni'n dysgu Cymraeg yn y* **dosbarth.**
We learn Welsh in class.

Dosbarth babanod   *Infants class*
Mae Ifan yn 7 ac mae o yn y **dosbarth babanod.**
Ifan is 7 and he is in the **infants' class.**

Dosbarth derbyn   *Reception class*
Mae Elin yn 5 ac mae hi yn y **dosbarth derbyn.**
Elin is 5 and she is in the **reception class.**

Dosbarth nos   *Night class*
Dan ni'n dysgu Cymraeg mewn **dosbarth nos.**
We are learning Welsh in a **night class.**

Drama *[eb]*
> dramâu

Play, drama

*Mi wnes i fynd i gysgu yn y **ddrama** – roedd hi'n ddiflas iawn.*

*I went to sleep in the **play** – it was very boring.*

Dringo

To climb

*Mi fyddwn ni'n **dringo**'r mynydd fory.*

*We will be **climbing** the mountain tomorrow.*

Dros

Over + Treiglad Meddal

*Maen nhw'n byw **dros** y bont.*

*They live **over** the bridge.*

*Mi wnes i fynd **dros** **B**ont Hafren.*

*I went **over** the Severn Bridge.*

Drwg

(i) Bad / Naughty

*Mae plant Aberheli yn **ddrwg** iawn.*

*The Aberheli children are very **naughty / bad**.*

(ii) Sorry

***Mae'n ddrwg iawn gen i** ond dw i ddim yn dallt.*

***I'm very sorry** but I don't understand.*

Drws *[eg]*
> drysau

Door

*Mi wnaethon ni fynd trwy'r **drws** i mewn i'r tŷ.*

*We went through the **door** into the house.*

Drws ffrynt / cefn *Front / Back door*

*Dach chi'n mynd i mewn trwy'r **drws ffrynt** ac allan trwy'r **drws cefn**.*

*You go in through the **front door** and out through the **back door**.*

Du

Black

*Dw i'n licio yfed coffi **du**, heb lefrith.*

*I like drinking **black** coffee, without milk.*

Dŵad	*To come [Standard Welsh: **Dod**]*
	*O le dach chi'n **dŵad** yn wreiddiol?*
	Where do you come *from originally?*
Dŵad â	*To bring [Standard Welsh: **Dod â**]*
	*Maen nhw'n **dŵad â**'r anrheg efo nhw.*
	*They're **bringing** the present with them.*
Dweud	*To say [Standard Welsh]*
	See > **Deud**
Dweud wrth	*To tell [Standard Welsh]*
	See > **Deud wrth**
Dŵr *[eg]*	*Water*
	*Roedd **dŵr** yr afon yn oer iawn.*
	*The **water** from the river was very cold.*
Dwylo	*See >* **Llaw**
Dwyrain *[eg]*	*East*
	*Mae'r haul yn codi yn y **dwyrain**.*
	*The sun rises in the **east**.*
Dy [+ di]	*Your [informal singular] + Treiglad Meddal*
	*Wnest ti ddŵad i'r dosbarth yn **dy** gar di?*
	*Did you come to class in **your** car?*
Dydd *[eg]*	*Day [See also: individual days of the week]*
> dyddiau	*Dan ni'n mynd i'r dosbarth bob **dydd**.*
	*We go to class every **day**.*
Dyfalu*	*To guess*
Dyma	*(i) Here is / are + Treiglad Meddal*
	***Dyma** lyfr da am arddio.*
	***Here's** a good book about gardening.*
	(ii) This is [introducing someone] + Treiglad Meddal
	***Dyma** fy mam.*
	***This is** my mother.*
Dyn *[eg]*	*Man*
> dynion	*Pwy ydy'r **dyn** newydd yn y dosbarth?*
	*Who is the new **man** in class?*

Dyna	*(i) There is / are + Treiglad Meddal*
	Dyna *ni.*
	There *we* **are.**
	(ii) How + adjective + Treiglad Meddal
	Dyna dd*iflas!*
	How *miserable!*
	(iii) That is + Treiglad Meddal
	Dyna f*am y plentyn.*
	That's *the child's mother.*
Dynes *[eb]*	*Woman*
	Pwy ydy'r **ddynes** *newydd yn y dosbarth?*
	Who is the new **woman** *in the class?*
Dysgu	*To learn [Also: to teach]*
	Dan ni'n **dysgu** *Cymraeg yn y dosbarth.*
	We **learn** *Welsh in class.*
	Mae'r tiwtor yn **dysgu** *Cymraeg i ni.*
	The tutor is **teaching** *us Welsh.*
Dysgwr *[eg]*	*Learner*
Dysgwraig *[eb]*	*[Female] Learner*
> dysgwyr	*Siaradwch yn araf, os gwelwch yn dda,* **dysgwr** *dw i.*
	Speak slowly, please, I am a **learner.**
	Dysgwraig *o Gasnewydd ydy Elin.*
	Elin is a **female learner** *from Newport.*

DD

Ddoe	*Yesterday*
	Mi wnes i fynd i siopa yn y dre **ddoe.**
	I went shopping in town **yesterday.**

E

E-bost	*E-mail*
	Mi wnes i gael e-bost am y cwrs newydd.
	I received an e-mail about the new course.
E-bostio	*To e-mail*
	Dw i'n e-bostio fy nhiwtor am y gwaith cartre.
	I am e-mailing my tutor about the homework.
Ebrill *[mis]*	*April*
	Mis rhif pedwar ydy mis Ebrill.
	April *is month number four.*
Echdoe	*The day before yesterday*
	Roedd hi'n oer iawn echdoe.
	It was very cold the day before (yesterday).
Edrych (ar)	*To look (at) / Watch*
	Mae'r ci'n edrych yn hapus.
	The dog looks happy.
	Mi fyddwn ni'n edrych ar y teledu heno.
	We will be watching / looking at the television tonight.
Efallai	*Perhaps [Standard Welsh]*
	See > Ella
Efo	*With [Standard Welsh: Gyda]*
	Dowch efo ni i'r dafarn!
	Come with us to the pub!
Eglwys *[eb]*	*Church*
> eglwysi	*Maen nhw'n mynd i'r eglwys bob dydd Sul.*
	They go to church every Sunday.
Ei *[benywaidd]*	*Her + Treiglad Llaes / H- before vowels*
	Mae Laura'n cael ei pharti pen-blwydd heddiw.
	Laura's having her birthday party today.

Mae hi'n licio **ei h**anrhegion hi.
*She likes **her** presents.*

Ei *[gwrywaidd]* *His* + Treiglad Meddal

*Mae o'n cael **ei b**arti pen-blwydd heddiw.*
*He's having **his** birthday party today.*

Eich *Your [formal singular / plural and informal plural]*

*Ydy **eich** plant chi'n mynd i ysgol Gymraeg?*
*Do **your** children go to a Welsh (language) school?*

Ein *Our + H- before vowels*

*Mae **ein** tŷ ni yng nghanol y dre.*
***Our** house is in the middle of town.*

*Diolch yn fawr am **ein h**anrheg ni.*
*Thanks very much for **our** present.*

Eira *[eg]* *Snow*

*(i) Mae popeth yn wyn efo'r **eira** i gyd.*
*Everything is white with all the **snow**.*

*(ii) Roedd hi'n **bwrw eira** yn yr Alban neithiwr.*
*It was **snowing** in Scotland last night.*

Eisiau *To want [Standard Welsh]*

*See > **Isio***

Eistedd *To sit*

*Roeddwn i'n **eistedd** yn y dosbarth am ddwy awr.*
*I was **sitting** in class for two hours.*

Eisteddfod *[eb]* *Eisteddfod*
> eisteddfodau *Mi fydd yr **eisteddfod** yn dŵad i'r gogledd eleni.*
*The **eisteddfod** will be coming to the north this year.*

Eitha *Quite*

*Mae hi'n **eitha** oer yn y neuadd.*
*It's **quite** cold in the hall.*

Eleni	*This year*
	*Lle dach chi'n mynd ar eich gwyliau **eleni**?*
	*Where are you going on your holidays **this year**?*
Ella	*Perhaps [Standard Welsh: **Efallai**]*
	***Ella** bydd o'n cyrraedd heddiw.*
	***Perhaps** he'll be arriving today.*
Ennill	*To win*
	*Pwy fydd yn **ennill** y rygbi eleni?*
	*Who will **win** the rugby this year?*
	*Y llynedd, mi wnaeth Cymru **ennill**.*
	*Last year, Wales **won**.*
Enw *[eg]*	*Name*
> enwau	*Be' ydy eich **enw** chi?*
	*What's your **name**?*
Enwog	*Famous*
	*Mae Anthony Hopkins yn actor **enwog**.*
	*Anthony Hopkins is a **famous** actor.*
Erbyn	*By [especially with time]*
	*Dowch i'r parti **erbyn** wyth o'r gloch.*
	*Come to the party **by** eight o'clock.*
Erbyn hyn	*By now*
	Erbyn hyn, *mae pawb wedi mynd.*
	*Everybody's gone **by now**.*
(Yn) erbyn	*Against*
	*Y gêm fawr ydy Cymru **yn erbyn** Lloegr.*
	*The big game is Wales **against** England.*
Erioed	*Ever, never*
	*Dw i **erioed** wedi gweld Pobol y Cwm.*
	*I've **never** seen Pobol y Cwm.*
	*Dach chi wedi gweld Pobol y Cwm **erioed**?*
	*Have you **ever** seen Pobol y Cwm?*

Ers *Since*
*Dw i'n aros yma **ers** naw o'r gloch.*
I am waiting (= I've been waiting) here
***since** nine o'clock.*

Ers pryd / faint? *Since when / How long*
Ers pryd / ers faint *dach chi'n aros yma?*
***(Since when) How long** have you been*
waiting here?

Esgusodwch fi! *Excuse me!*
Esgusodwch fi! *Lle mae'r dosbarth Cymraeg?*
***Excuse me!** Where is the Welsh class?*

Eto *(i) Yet*
*Dydy hi ddim wedi gwneud y gwaith **eto**.*
*She hasn't done the work **yet**.*
(ii) Again [See > **Unwaith***]*

Eu *Their + H- before vowels*
*Mae **eu** car nhw yn y maes parcio.*
***Their** car is in the car park.*
*Faint ydy **eu h**oed nhw?*
*What is **their** age? / How old are they?*

Ewythr *[eg]* *Uncle [Also:* **Wncwl***]*
> ewythredd *Doedd fy **ewythr** ddim yn medru siarad*
Cymraeg.
*My **uncle** couldn't speak Welsh.*

F

Faint?	*How much? How many?*
	Faint *o blant sy yn y dosbarth?*
	How many *children are in the class?*
	Faint *o'r gloch ydy hi?*
	What time is it? (lit: **How much** *o'clock is it?)*
Fe / e	*He [Standard Welsh]*
	See > **Fo**
Fel	*(i) Like*
	Mae'r mab yn edrych **fel** *ei dad.*
	The son looks **like** *his father.*
	(ii) As
	Mae hi'n gweithio **fel** *athrawes.*
	She works **as** *a teacher.*
Fel arfer	*Usually*
	Mae'r dosbarth yn gorffen am naw **fel arfer**.
	The class **usually** *finishes at nine.*
Fi / i	*(i) Me, I*
	Fi *ydy'r person cynta i gyrraedd.*
	I'm / **It's me** *who is the first person to arrive.*
	> [NW also: **'mi'** *after the preposition* **'i'** *= to]*
	Rhaid i **mi** *roi'r pres i Siôn.*
	I must give the money to Siôn (lit: there's a need **to me** *to give the money to Siôn).*
	Esgusodwch **fi**!
	Excuse **me**!
	(ii) My [+ fy]
	Mae fy nhad i wedi prynu tŷ newydd.
	My *father has bought a new house.*

Fideo *[eg]* *Video*
> fideos *Maen nhw'n gwneud **fideo** o gyngerdd yr ysgol.*
*They are making a **video** of the school concert.*

Fo / o *(i) He [Standard Welsh:* **Fe**]
*Roedd **o**'n chwarae pêl-droed.*
He *was playing football.*
(ii) His [+ ei]
*Be' ydy ei gyfeiriad **o**?*
*What is **his** address?*

Fy *My + Treiglad Trwynol*
*Mae **fy ngh**ar i wedi torri i lawr.*
My *car has broken down.*

FF

Ffatri *[eb]* *Factory*
> ffatrïoedd *Mi fydd y **ffatri**'n cau yn yr haf.*
*The **factory** will be closing in the summer.*

Ffeil *[eb]* *File*
> ffeiliau *Dw i wedi colli fy **ffeil** gwaith cartre.*
*I've lost my homework **file**.*

Ffenest[r] *[eb]* *Window*
> ffenestri *Agorwch y **ffenest** – mae'n boeth yma!*
*Open the **window** – it's hot here!*

Fferm *[eb]* *Farm*
> ffermydd *Maen nhw'n cadw llawer o anifeiliaid ar y **fferm**.*
*They keep many animals on the **farm**.*

Ffermio *To farm*
*Mae 'na lawer o bobl yng Nghymru yn **ffermio**.*
*Many people in Wales **farm**.*

Ffermwr *[eg]*
> ffermwyr

Farmer
*Does gan y **ffermwr** ddim llawer o bres.*
*The **farmer** hasn't got a lot of money.*

Ffilm *[eb]*
> ffilmiau

Film
Ffilm *Gymraeg ydy* Hedd Wyn.
Hedd Wyn *is a Welsh (language)* **film**.

Fflat *[eb]*
> fflatiau

Flat
*Roedden nhw'n byw mewn **fflat** yng nghanol y dre.*
*They were living in a **flat** in the middle of town.*

Bloc o fflatiau

A block of flats
*Roedden nhw'n byw mewn **bloc o fflatiau** yng nghanol y dre.*
*They were living in a **block of flats** in the middle of town.*

Ffliw *[eg]*

Flu
*Roedd hi'n sâl iawn – roedd gynni hi **ffliw**.*
*She was very ill – she had **flu**.*

Ffôn *[eg]*
> ffonau

Phone [noun]

Ffôn symudol

Mobile phone
*Mi wnaeth hi golli ei **ffôn symudol** newydd.*
*She lost her new **mobile phone**.*

Rhif ffôn

Phone number
*Be' ydy eich **rhif ffôn** chi?*
*What's your **phone number**?*

Ffonio

To phone
*Mae Aled yn mynd i **ffonio** pawb yn y dosbarth.*
*Aled's going to **phone** everyone in the class.*

Ffordd *[eb]*
> ffyrdd

(i) Way
 *Maen nhw ar y **ffordd** i'r dosbarth.*
They are on the way to class.
(ii) Road
*Mi wnaeth y car stopio yng nghanol y **ffordd**.*
The car stopped in the middle of the road.

Ffrainc
France
*Dan ni'n hoff iawn o win o **Ffrainc**.*
We're very fond of wine from France.

Ffrind *[eg]*
> **ffrindiau**

Friend
*Mae Ieuan yn **ffrind** da i mi...*
Ieuan is a good friend to me...

Ffrind gorau
Best friend
*... ond Iestyn ydy fy **ffrind gorau**.*
... but Iestyn is my best friend.

G

Gadael
To leave, depart
*Am faint o'r gloch mae'r trên yn **gadael** yr orsaf?*
What time does the train leave / depart from the station?

Gaea *[eg]*
Winter
*Weithiau, mae'n bwrw eira yn y **gaea**.*
Sometimes, it snows in winter.

Gair *[eg]*
> geiriau

Word
*Mi wnes i ddallt pob **gair** yn y rhaglen.*
I understood every word in the programme.

Galw
To call
*Mi fydd Dafydd yn **galw** ar ôl ei ddosbarth.*
Dafydd will be calling after his class.

Gallu	*To be able to / Can [Standard Welsh]*
	See > **Medru**
Gan	*Used to form the 'have / got' construction =*
	'with'
	Mae **gan** *Catrin ddau o blant.*
	Catrin **has got** two children [lit: There are
	two children **with** Catrin].
Gardd *[eb]*	*Garden*
> gerddi	*Maen nhw'n hapus yn eistedd yn yr* **ardd**.
	They're happy sitting in the **garden**.
Garddio	*To garden, to do the gardening*
	Doedd hi ddim yn licio **garddio**...
	She didn't like **gardening**...
Garddwr *[eg]*	*Gardener*
> garddwyr	*... felly mi wnaeth hi ffonio'r* **garddwr**.
	... so she phoned the **gardener**.
Garej *[eg]*	*Garage*
> garejys	*Mae'r car yn y* **garej** *heno.*
	The car is in the **garage** tonight.
	Dan ni'n mynd i'r **garej** *i brynu petrol.*
	We're going to the **garage** to buy petrol.
Geirfa *[eb]**	*Vocabulary*
Gêm *[eb]*	*Game*
> gemau	*Mi fydd y* **gêm** *rhwng Abertawe a Chaerdydd*
	yn bwysig iawn.
	The **game** between Swansea and Cardiff will
	be very important.
	Mae'r plant yn licio chwarae **gemau** *cyfrifiadur.*
	The children like playing computer **games**.
Genod	*See >* **Hogan**
Glanhau	*To clean [Standard Welsh]*
	See > **Llnau**
Glas	*Blue*
	Mae Siân yn gwisgo cardigan **las** *heddiw.*
	Siân is wearing a **blue** cardigan today.

Glaw *[eg]*   *Rain*
(i) Mae popeth yn wlyb iawn ar ôl y **glaw**.
Everything is very wet after the **rain**.
(ii) Roedd hi'n **bwrw glaw** *yn y gogledd neithiwr.*
It was **raining** *in the north last night.*

Gofyn (i)   *To ask*
Dw i isio **gofyn** *cwestiwn am y daflen waith.*
I want to **ask** *a question about the worksheet.*
Dw i'n mynd i **ofyn i**'*r tiwtor.*
I'm going to **ask** *the tutor.*

Gogledd *[eg]*   *North*
Mae pobl y **gogledd** *yn deud 'efo' am 'gyda'.*
The people from the **north** *say 'efo' for 'gyda'.*

Golchi   *To wash (something) [See >* **ymolchi** *for 'wash yourself']*
Wyt ti'n **golchi** *dy wallt heno?*
Are you **washing** *your hair tonight?*

Golff *[eg]*   *Golf*
Dw i'n mwynhau chwarae **golff** *bob dydd Sadwrn.*
I enjoy playing **golf** *every Saturday.*

Gorffen   *To finish*
(i) Dach chi wedi **gorffen** *bwyta eto?*
Have you **finished** *eating yet?*
(ii) Mi fydd y cwrs yn **gorffen** *mewn tair wythnos.*
The course will be **finishing** *in three weeks.*

Gorffennaf *[mis]* *July*
Mis rhif saith ydy mis **Gorffennaf**.
July *is month number seven.*

Gorllewin *[eg]*   *West*
Mae'r haul yn mynd i lawr yn y **gorllewin**.
The sun goes down in the **west**.

Gormod [o]   *Too much*
Dydy hi ddim isio pwdin. Mae hi wedi bwyta **gormod**.
She doesn't want pudding. She has eaten too much.
Maen nhw wedi yfed **gormod o** *win.*
They've drunk too much wine.

Gorsaf *[eb]*   *Station*
> gorsafoedd

Gorsaf betrol   *Petrol station*
Mae'r **orsaf betrol** *yn gwerthu popeth.*
The petrol station sells everything.

Gorsaf fysiau   *Bus station*
Mi fydda i'n teithio o **orsaf fysiau** *Port Talbot.*
I will be travelling from Port Talbot bus station.

Gorsaf dân   *Fire station*
Mi fydd **gorsaf dân** *newydd Pontypandy yng nghanol y dre.*
Pontypandy's new fire station will be in the middle of town.

Gorsaf drenau   *Train station*
Mae **gorsaf drenau** *Caerdydd yn agos i'r siopau.*
Cardiff train station is near to the shops.

Gorsaf yr heddlu   *Police station*
Mae'r plismon yn gweithio yng **ngorsaf yr heddlu.**
The policeman works in the police station.

Grŵp *[eg]*   *Group*
> grwpiau   *Mi fydd* **grŵp** *o ddysgwyr yn mynd i'r theatr heno.*
A group of learners will be going to the theatre tonight.

Gwaith grŵp	*Group work*
	*Mi fyddwn ni'n gwneud **gwaith grŵp** am hanner awr.*
	*We will be doing **group work** for half an hour.*
Gwaith *[eg]*	*Work [noun] [See also: Gweithio]*
	*Dan ni'n dysgu Cymraeg yn y **gwaith**.*
	*We are learning Welsh at **work**.*
	*Ydy'r **gwaith** yn talu am y cwrs?*
	*Is **work** paying for the course?*
Gwaith cartre	*Homework*
	*Cofiwch wneud eich **gwaith cartre** heno!*
	*Remember to do your **homework** tonight!*
Gwallt *[eg]*	*Hair*
	*Mae gynni hi **wallt** hir, du.*
	*She's got long, black **hair**.*
Gwanwyn *[eg]*	*Spring*
	*Mae'r **gwanwyn** yn dŵad ar ôl y gaea.*
	***Spring** comes after winter.*
Gwddf *[eg]* / **Gwddw** *[eg]* *Throat, neck*	
> gyddfau	*Roedd gan y plant ddolur **gwddw**.*
	*The children had a sore **throat**.*
Gweddol	*Rather, fairly + Treiglad Meddal*
	*Mi fydd hi'n **weddol b**oeth y prynhawn yma.*
	*It will be **fairly** hot this afternoon.*
Gweithio	*To work*
	*Mae Gwen yn **gweithio** fel nyrs yn Ysbyty Bronglais.*
	*Gwen **works** as a nurse at Bronglais Hospital.*
	*Dydy'r peiriant ddim yn **gweithio**.*
	*The machine doesn't **work**.*
Gweithiwr *[eg]*	*Worker*
> gweithwyr	***Gweithiwr** mewn ffatri ydy Aled.*
	*Aled is a **worker** in a factory.*

Gweld   *To see*
*Dw i ddim wedi **gweld** Megan ers wythnosau.*
I haven't seen Megan for weeks.

Gwely *[eg]*   *Bed*
> gwelyau   *Mae'r plentyn yn cysgu'n braf yn y **gwely**.*
The child is sleeping well / sound asleep in bed.

Gwener, dydd   *Friday*
*Dw i'n licio **dydd Gwener** – dw i'n gadael y gwaith yn gynnar.*
I like Friday – I leave work early.

Nos Wener   *Friday night*
*Maen nhw'n mynd allan bob **nos Wener**.*
They go out every Friday night.

Gwerthu   *To sell*
*Dan ni isio symud ond dan ni ddim wedi **gwerthu**'r tŷ eto.*
We want to move but we haven't sold the house yet.

Gwesty *[eg]*   *Hotel*
> gwestai   *Mi fyddwn ni'n aros mewn **gwesty** ar ein gwyliau.*
We will be staying in a hotel on our holidays.

Gwin *[eg]*   *Wine*
> gwinoedd   *Dw i'n cael cur pen ar ôl yfed **gwin** coch.*
I get a headache after drinking red wine.

Gwir   *(i) True*
*Ydy'r stori yma'n **wir**?*
Is this story true?
(ii) Indeed
Wir *i chi!*
Absolutely! / Really! *[lit: Indeed to you]*

Gwirion   *Stupid*
*Roedd y dyn yn deud llawer o bethau **gwirion**.*
The man was saying lots of stupid things.

Gwisgo   *To wear, dress*
*Rhaid i chi **wisgo** eich côt – mae'n oer heddiw.*
You must wear your coat – it's cold today.

Gwlad *[eb]*   *Country*
> gwledydd   *Mae Cymru'n **wlad** fach.*
Wales is a small country.

Cefn gwlad   *Countryside*
*Mi wnaethon nhw symud o Gaerdydd i **gefn gwlad** Cymru.*
They moved from Cardiff to the Welsh countryside.

Gwlyb   *Wet*
*Ar ôl y glaw, roedden ni i gyd yn **wlyb** iawn.*
After the rain, we were all very wet.

Gwneud   *(i) To do*
*Dach chi wedi **gwneud** yn dda yn y gwaith.*
You have done well at work.
(ii) To make
*Mi fydda i'n **gwneud** swper heno.*
I will be making dinner tonight.

Gŵr *[eg]*   *Husband*
> gwŷr   **Gŵr** *Mair ydy Alun.*
Alun is Mair's husband.

Gwraig *[eb]*   *Wife*
> gwragedd   **Gwraig** *Alun ydy Mair.*
Mair is Alun's wife.

Gŵr / Gwraig tŷ *House-husband / Housewife*
*Mae Glyn yn gwneud y gwaith tŷ – **gŵr tŷ** ydy o.*
Glyn does the housework – he's a house-husband.

	Mae Sioned yn gwneud y gwaith tŷ – **gwraig tŷ** *ydy hi.*
	Sioned does the housework – she's a **housewife**.
Gwrando [ar]	*To listen (to)*
	Bob bore, dw i'n **gwrando ar** *y radio.*
	Every morning, I **listen to** the radio.
	Be' wnaethoch chi ddeud? Doeddwn i ddim yn **gwrando**.
	What did you say? I wasn't **listening**.
Gwreiddiol	*Originally*
	Mae Anthony Hopkins yn dŵad o Fargam, Port Talbot, **yn wreiddiol**.
	Anthony Hopkins comes from Margam, Port Talbot, **originally**.
Gwrywaidd*	*Masculine (*Enw gwrywaidd *= Masculine noun)*
Gwybod	*To know [a fact, something]*
	Dw i ddim yn **gwybod** *lle mae hi'n byw.*
	I don't **know** where she lives.
Gŵyl Dewi, dydd	Saint David's day
	Mae **dydd Gŵyl Dewi** *ar 1 Mawrth bob blwyddyn.*
	St David's day is on 1 March every year.
Gwyliau	*Holidays*
	Mi wnaethon ni fynd i Sbaen ar ein **gwyliau**.
	We went to Spain on our **holidays**.
Gwylio	*To view, to watch*
	Wyt ti'n **gwylio** *S4C?*
	Do you **watch** S4C?
Gwyn	*White*
	Dw i'n yfed coffi **gwyn** *efo digon o lefrith.*
	I drink **white** coffee with enough / plenty of milk.

Gwynt [eg]	*Wind*
> gwyntoedd	*Mae **gwynt** y gogledd yn oer iawn.*
	*The north **wind** is very cold.*
Gwyntog	*Windy*
	*Roedd hi'n **wyntog** iawn neithiwr.*
	*It was very **windy** last night.*
Gwyrdd	*Green*
	*Mae hi'n licio bag **gwyrdd** ei ffrind.*
	*She likes her friend's **green** bag.*
Gyda	*With [Standard Welsh]*
	*See > **Efo***
Gyferbyn [â]	*Opposite*
	*Maen nhw'n byw **gyferbyn** â'r siopau.*
	*They live **opposite** the shops.*
Gyrru	*To drive*
	*Pwy sy'n **gyrru**'r car heno?*
	*Who's **driving** the car tonight?*
Gyrrwr [eg]	*Driver*
> gyrwyr	***Gyrrwr** tacsi ydy Ffred.*
	*Ffred is a taxi **driver**.*

H

Haf *[eg]*	*Summer*
	*Mae'r **haf** yn dwad ar ôl y gwanwyn.*
	***Summer** comes after spring.*
Halen *[eg]*	*Salt*
	*Mae gormod o **halen** yn ddrwg i chi.*
	*Too much **salt** is bad for you.*
	*Pupur a **halen**.*
	*Pepper and **salt**.*

Hamdden *[eb]* *Leisure*
Be' dach chi'n wneud yn eich amser
hamdden?
*What do you do in your **leisure** time?*

Hanner *[eg]* *Half*
*Mi fydda i'n cael **hanner** peint yn y dafarn heno.*
*I'll be having **half** a pint in the pub tonight.*
*Mae hi'n **hanner** awr wedi chwech.*
*It's **half** past six.*

Hapus *Happy*
*Mi wnaeth Gareth ennill £5,000 [pum mil o bunnoedd] – roedd o'n **hapus** iawn!*
*Gareth won £5,000 – he was very **happy**!*

Haul *[eg]* *Sun*
*Roedd hi'n braf gweld yr **haul** bob dydd yn Sbaen.*
*It was lovely to see the **sun** every day in Spain.*

Heb *Without + Treiglad Meddal*
*Mi wnes i ddŵad i'r dosbarth **heb g**ôt y bore yma.*
*I came to class **without** a coat this morning.*

Hedfan *To fly*
*Mi fyddwn ni'n **hedfan** o Heathrow i Las Vegas.*
*We will be **flying** from Heathrow to Las Vegas.*

Heddiw *Today*
*Mae hi'n braf **heddiw** ond mi fydd hi'n wlyb fory.*
*It's fine **today** but it will be wet tomorrow.*

Heddlu *[eg]* *Police*
*Ffoniwch 999 [naw naw naw] a gofynnwch am yr **heddlu**.*
*Phone 999 and ask for the **police**.*

Hefyd	*Also, as well, too*
	*Dach chi'n dŵad i'r dafarn **hefyd**?*
	Are you coming to the pub as well / too?
Help [eg]	*Help*
	*Mae'r gwaith cartre'n anodd – dach chi'n medru rhoi **help** i mi?*
	The homework is difficult – can you give me help [lit: give help to me]?
Helpu	*To help*
	*Mi fydd y tiwtor yn **helpu**'r dosbarth efo'r gwaith cartre.*
	The tutor will help the class with the homework.
Hen	*Old*
	*Dydy 75 [saith deg pump] ddim yn **hen** y dyddiau yma.*
	75 isn't old these days.
Heno	*Tonight*
	*Dw i ddim yn medru mynd i'r cyngerdd **heno**.*
	I can't go to the concert tonight.
Het [eb]	*Hat*
> hetiau	*Gwisgwch **het** – mae hi'n oer iawn heddiw.*
	Wear a hat – it's very cold today.
Heulog	*Sunny*
	*Roedd hi'n **heulog** bob dydd ar ein gwyliau.*
	It was sunny every day on our holidays.
Hi	*(i) She*
	*Roedd **hi**'n chwarae pêl-droed.*
	She was playing football.
	(ii) her [+ ei]
	*Be' ydy ei chyfeiriad **hi**?*
	What is her address?
Hir	*Long*
	*Mae'n ffordd **hir** i Madrid.*
	It's a long way to Madrid.

Hoci *[eg]*   *Hockey*
*Doeddwn i ddim yn licio chwarae **hoci** yn yr ysgol.*
*I didn't like playing **hockey** at school.*

Hoci iâ   *Ice hockey*
*Maen nhw'n chwarae **hoci iâ** yn Toronto.*
*They play **ice hockey** in Toronto.*

Hoffi [Licio]   *To like*
*Dw i'n **hoffi** pasta ond dw i ddim yn **hoffi** cyrri.*
*I **like** pasta but I don't **like** curry.*

Hogan *[eb]*   *Girl [Standard Welsh: **Merch**]*
> genod
*Fel **hogan** fach, dw i'n cofio chwarae hoci yn yr ysgol.*
*As a small **girl**, I remember playing hockey at school.*

Hogyn   *Boy [Standard Welsh: **Bachgen**]*
> hogiau
*Fel **hogyn** bach, dw i'n cofio chwarae pêl-droed ar y stryd.*
*[As a small **boy**, I remember playing football in the street]*

Hon   *This [feminine]*
*Mae **hon** yn gêm dda.*
This *is a good game.*
*Siân ydy **hon**…*
This *is Siân…*

Honna   *That [feminine]*
*… ac Elin ydy **honna**.*
*… and **that's** Elin.*

Hufen iâ *[eg]*   *Ice cream*
*Roedd hi'n braf bwyta **hufen iâ** yn yr haul.*
*It was lovely eating **ice cream** in the sun.*

Hwn
This [masculine]
*Tŷ mawr ydy **hwn**.*
This *is a big house.*
*Gareth ydy **hwn**...*
This *is Gareth...*

Hwnna / Hwnnw *That [masculine]*
*... ac Aled ydy **hwnna**.*
*... and **that's** Aled.*

Hwyl *[eb]*
> hwyliau
Fun
*Mi wnaethon ni gael llawer o **hwyl** yn y dosbarth.*
*We had lots of **fun** in class.*

Pob hwyl
All the best, goodbye
Pob hwyl i chi am y tro!
All the best for the time being! / **Bye** for now!

Hwyr
Late
*Mae hi bob amser yn cyrraedd yn **hwyr**.*
*She always arrives **late**.*

Hydref
Autumn
*Mae'r **hydref** yn dŵad ar ôl yr haf.*
Autumn *comes after summer.*

Hydref *[mis]*
October
*Mis rhif deg ydy mis **Hydref**.*
October *is month number ten.*

Hyfryd
Lovely, pleasant
*Roedd yn **hyfryd** gweld Elwyn eto.*
*It was **lovely** to see Elwyn again.*

Hysbyseb *[eb]*
> hysbysebion
Advert[isement]
*Dw i ddim yn gwylio'r **hysbysebion** ar y teledu.*
*I don't watch the **adverts** on the television.*

I

I	(i) *To / For* + *Treiglad Meddal*
	Dan ni'n mynd **i b**arti yn nhŷ Elin heno.
	We're going to *a party in Elin's house*
	tonight.
	Be' dach chi'n mynd **i w**neud fory?
	What are you going to *do tomorrow?*
	Be' wnest ti gael **i g**inio?
	What did you have for *lunch?*
	(ii) *I / me*
	Dw **i** *wedi gorffen y gwaith erbyn hyn.*
	I *have finished the work by now.*
	Rhowch y pres **i** *mi!*
	Give the money to *me! / Give me the money!*

I fyny	*Up*
	Maen nhw'n byw **i fyny** *ar y mynydd.*
	They live **up** *on the mountain.*

I ffwrdd	*Away, off*
	Mi wnaethon ni fynd **i ffwrdd** *am wythnos o wyliau.*
	We went **away** *for a week's holiday.*

| I ffwrdd â chi! | **Off** *with you!* |

I gyd	*All* [always comes after the noun]
	Mae'r plant **i gyd** *yn siarad Cymraeg.*
	All *the children speak Welsh.*

I lawr	*Down*
	Mi wnaethon ni gerdded **i lawr** *y mynydd.*
	We walked **down** *the mountain.*
	Mae fy nghar wedi torri **i lawr**.
	My car has broken **down**.

Iau, dydd *Thursday*
*Dw i'n mynd i siopa yn y dre bob **dydd** Iau.*
*I go shopping in town every **Thursday**.*

Nos Iau *Thursday night*
*Maen nhw'n mynd i'r sinema **nos** Iau.*
*They are going to the cinema on **Thursday night**.*

Iawn *(i) OK, alright*
*Ydy popeth yn **iawn**?*
*Is everything **OK / alright**?*
(ii) Very [after the adjective]
*Yn y gaea, mae'r tŷ yma'n oer **iawn**.*
*In the winter, this house is **very** cold.*

Iechyd *[eg]* *Health*
*Sut mae eich **iechyd** chi erbyn hyn?*
*How is your **health** by now?*
Iechyd da!
*Good **health**! / Cheers!*

Ifanc *Young*
*Mae 'na lawer o bobl **ifanc** yn ein dosbarth ni.*
*There are many **young** people in our class.*

Ionawr *[mis]* *January*
*Mis **Ionawr** ydy mis cynta'r flwyddyn.*
***January** is the first month of the year.*

Isio *To want [Standard Welsh: **Eisiau**]*
*Dw i **isio** dysgu'r geiriau newydd.*
*I **want** to learn the new words.*

Isio diod *Thirsty [lit: want a drink]*
*Maen nhw'n prynu potel o ddŵr. Maen nhw **isio diod**.*
*They're buying a bottle of water. They're **thirsty** / They **want a drink**.*

J

Jam *[eg]*
Jam
*Dw i isio brechdan **jam** i de.*
I want a jam sandwich for tea.

L

Ledled
All over, across
*Mi fydd y grŵp yn teithio **ledled** Cymru.*
The group will be travelling all over Wales.

Lemon *[eg]*
> lemonau
Lemon
*Maen nhw'n yfed te efo **lemon**.*
They're drinking tea with lemon.

Licio
*To like [Other variant: **Hoffi**]*
*Dw i'n **licio** pasta ond dw i ddim yn **licio** cyrri.*
I like pasta but I don't like curry.

Lifft *[eg]*
> lifftiau
Lift (i) = in a building
*Dydy'r **lifft** ddim yn mynd yn gyflym iawn.*
The lift doesn't go very fast.
(ii) = ride
*Dach chi'n medru rhoi **lifft** i mi i'r dre?*
Can you give me a lift into town?

Lobsgows
Soup, broth, 'lobsgows'
*Mae'r plant yn licio bwyta **lobsgows** a bara cartre.*
The children like eating lobscows and home-made bread.

Lolfa *[eb]*
Lounge
*Dw i'n edrych ar y teledu yn y **lolfa**.*
I'm watching television in the lounge.

Losin *[ell]*   *Sweets [Other variants:* **Da-da, Fferins, Petha da***]*
Dydy bwyta gormod o **losin** *ddim yn dda i'ch dannedd.*
Eating too many **sweets** *is not good for your teeth.*

LL

Llaeth *[eg]*   *Milk [Standard Welsh]*
See > **Llefrith**
Llaw *[eb]*   *Hand*
> dwylo   *Mae hi'n ysgrifennu efo'r* **llaw** *dde.*
She writes with her right **hand** */ She's right-*
hand*ed.*
Golchwch eich **dwylo** *cyn bwyta!*
Wash your **hands** *before eating!*
Llawer (o)   *Many, much, a lot [of], lots of*
Mae **llawer** *yn mynd ymlaen yma.*
There's **a lot / much** *going on here.*
Mi fydd 'na **lawer** *o bobl yn y cyfarfod.*
There will be **many / lots of** *people in the meeting.*
Lle *[eg]*   *Place*
> lleoedd   *Mae'n* **lle** *da iawn i gael peint a siarad Cymraeg.*
It's a very good **place** *to have a pint and speak Welsh.*
Lle?   *Where? [Standard Welsh:* **Ble?***]*
Lle *mae Siân a Dafydd yn byw?*
Where *do Siân and Dafydd live?*
Lle chwech   *Toilet [Other variant:* **tŷ bach***]*
Lle mae'r **lle chwech***, os gwelwch yn dda?*
Where's the **toilet** *please?*

Llefrith *[eg]*   *Milk [Standard Welsh:* **Llaeth***]*
                  Dach chi'n cymryd **llefrith** *yn eich te?*
                  Do you take **milk** *in your tea?*

Llenwi bylchau* *Filling in the gaps*

Llestri *[ell]*   *Dishes*
                  Pwy sy'n golchi'r **llestri** *heno?*
                  Who's washing the **dishes** *tonight?*

Lliw *[eg]*   *Colour*
> lliwiau   *Be' ydy* **lliw** *eich car chi?*
                  What's the **colour** *of your car? / What*
                  colour *is your car?*

Llnau   *To clean [Standard Welsh:* **Glanhau***]*
                  Mi fydda i'n **llnau**'*r tŷ ddydd Sadwrn.*
                  I will be **cleaning** *the house on Saturday.*

Lloegr *[eb]*   *England*
                  Mae Birmingham a Windsor yn **Lloegr.**
                  Birmingham and Windsor are in **England.**

Llun *[eg]*   *Picture*
> lluniau   *Be' ydy gwaith y dyn yn y* **llun***?*
                  What's the work of the man in the **picture***?*
                  / What does the man in the **picture** *do?*

Llun, dydd   *Monday*
                  Dw i'n mynd yn ôl i'r gwaith bob **dydd Llun.**
                  I go back to work every **Monday.**

Nos Lun   *Monday night*
                  Dydyn nhw ddim yn mynd allan **nos Lun.**
                  They don't go out on **Monday night.**

Lluosog*   *Plural*

Llwyd   *Grey*
                  Mae gan Robyn wallt **llwyd.**
                  Robyn's got **grey** *hair.*

Llyfr *[eg]*   *Book*
> llyfrau   *Dan ni'n darllen **llyfr** da am Tom Jones.*
                          *We're reading a good **book** about Tom Jones.*

Llyfr cwrs   *Course book*
                          *Dw i byth yn mynd i'r dosbarth heb fy **llyfr cwrs**.*
                          *I never go to my class without my **course book**.*

Llygad *[eg]*   *Eye*
> llygaid   *Dan ni'n gweld efo ein **llygaid**.*
                          *We see with our **eyes**.*

Llynedd (y)   *Last year*
                          *Y **llynedd**, mi wnaethon ni fynd i Ffrainc ar*
                          ein gwyliau.
                          ***Last year**, we went to France on our holidays.*

Llysiau *[ell]*   *Vegetables*
                          *Dan ni'n licio bwyta **llysiau** o'r ardd.*
                          *We like eating **vegetables** from the garden.*

Llysieuwr *[eg]*   *Vegetarian (man)*
> llysieuwyr

Llysieuwraig *[eb]* *Vegetarian (woman)*

> llysieuwragedd **Llysieuwr** *ydy Twm: dydy o ddim yn bwyta*
                          cig.
                          *Twm is a **vegetarian**: he doesn't eat meat.*
                          ***Llysieuwraig** ydy Myfanwy: dydy hi ddim*
                          yn bwyta cig.
                          *Myfanwy is a **vegetarian**: she doesn't eat*
                          meat.

Llythyr *[eg]*   *Letter [i.e. through the post]*
> llythyrau   *Dach chi wedi cael y **llythyr** eto?*
                          *Have you had the **letter** yet?*

M

Mab *[eg]*   *Son*
> meibion

*Mae gen i dri **mab** ac maen nhw'n byw yn Llandrindod.*

*I have three **sons** and they live in Llandrindod Wells.*

Mab yng nghyfraith *Son-in-law*

*Enw fy **mab yng nghyfraith** (gŵr fy merch) ydy Alun.*

*My **son-in-law** (my daughter's husband)'s name is Alun.*

Maes parcio *[eg]* *Car park*
> meysydd parcio *Mi wnaethon ni barcio ein car yn y **maes parcio**.*

*We parked our car in the **car park**.*

Mai *[mis]*   *May*

*Mis rhif pump ydy mis **Mai**.*

***May** is month number five.*

Mam *[eb]* / **Mami** *Mother / Mum*
> mamau *Mae hi'n byw efo'i **mam** yng Nghastell-nedd.*

*She lives with her **mother** in Neath.*

*Mi wnaeth **Mam** fynd i weld ei brawd yn y Rhyl.*

***Mam / Mum** went to see her brother in Rhyl.*

Mam yng nghyfraith *Mother-in-law*

*Enw fy **mam yng nghyfraith** (mam fy ngwraig) ydy Gwyneth.*

*My **mother-in-law** (my wife's mother)'s name is Gwyneth.*

Mawr   *Big, large*

*Enw fy mrawd **mawr** ydy Ifor.*

*The name of my **big** brother is Ifor.*

Yn fawr   *A lot, a great deal, very much*
*Diolch **yn fawr** iawn i chi.*
*Thank you **very much**.*
*Dw i'n licio **Pobol y Cwm** yn fawr.*
I like Pobol y Cwm **a lot / a great deal / very much**.

Mawrth, dydd   *Tuesday*
*Dw i'n cyfarfod ffrindiau bob **dydd Mawrth**.*
*I meet friends every **Tuesday**.*

Nos Fawrth   *Tuesday night*
*Maen nhw'n mynd i'r ganolfan hamdden **nos Fawrth**.*
*They are going to the leisure centre on **Tuesday night**.*

Mawrth [*mis*]   *March*
*Mis rhif tri ydy mis **Mawrth**.*
March *is month number three.*

Medi [*mis*]   *September*
*Mis rhif naw ydy mis **Medi**.*
September *is month number nine.*

Medru   *To be able to / can [Standard Welsh: **Gallu**]*
*Dw i ddim yn **medru** gweld y car.*
*I **can**'t see the car / I am not **able to** see the car.*

Meddwl (am)   *To think [about]*
*Mi fyddwn ni'n **meddwl** am ei syniad hi.*
*We will be **thinking** about her idea.*

Meddyg [*eg*]   *Doctor*
> meddygon   *Mi wnaeth Siôn fynd at y **meddyg** ar ôl torri ei fraich.*
*Siôn went to the **doctor** after breaking his arm.*

Meddygfa [*eb*]   *Surgery, medical centre*
*Mae **meddygfa** Cwm Sgwt yn agor am wyth o'r gloch.*
*Cwm Sgwt **surgery** opens at eight o'clock.*

Mehefin *[mis]*   *June*
Mis rhif chwech ydy mis **Mehefin**.
June *is month number six.*

Melyn   *Yellow*
Roedd hi'n gyrru car **melyn**.
She was driving a **yellow** *car.*

Menyn *[eg]*   *Butter*
Maen nhw'n licio **menyn** *ar eu bara.*
They like **butter** *on their bread.*

Merch *[eb]*   *(i) Daughter*
> merched   *Mae gen i dair* **merch** *ac maen nhw'n byw*
See > **Hogan**   *yn Wrecsam.*
I have three **daughters** *and they live in*
Wrexham.
(ii) Girl [Standard Welsh]

Merch yng nghyfraith   *Daughter-in-law*
Enw fy **merch yng nghyfraith** *(gwraig fy mab) ydy*
Alys.
My **daughter-in-law** *(my son's wife)'s name is Alys.*

Mercher, dydd   *Wednesday*
Dw i'n aros yn y tŷ bob **dydd Mercher**.
I stay in the house every **Wednesday**.

Nos Fercher   *Wednesday night*
Maen nhw'n chwarae tennis ar **nos Fercher**.
They play tennis on **Wednesday night**.

Mewn   *In a*
Maen nhw'n byw **mewn** *fflat yng nghanol y*
dre.
They live **in a** *flat in the middle of town.*

Mewn pryd   *In time*
Mi wnaethon ni gyrraedd y ddrama **mewn pryd**.
We arrived at the play **in time**.

72

Mis *[eg]* *Month*
> misoedd *Maen nhw'n chwarae golff bob **mis**.*
*They play golf every **month**.*

Modryb *[eb]* *Aunt, auntie [Also: **Anti**]*
> modrybedd *Doedd fy **modryb** ddim yn medru siarad Saesneg.*
*My **auntie** couldn't speak English.*

Môr *[eg]* *Sea*
> moroedd *Mae hi'n rhy oer i nofio yn y **môr**.*
*It's too cold to swim in the **sea**.*

Moron *[ell]* *Carrots*
*Mae'r **moron** wedi dŵad o'n gardd ni.*
*The **carrots** have come from our garden.*

Munud *[eg]* *Minute*
> munudau *Mae 60 [chwe deg] **munud** mewn awr.*
*There are 60 **minutes** in an hour.*
*Mi fydd y trên yn cyrraedd mewn pedwar **munud**.*
*The train will be arriving in four **minutes**.*

Mwy (o) *More*
*Dach chi isio **mwy o** siwgr?*
*Do you want **more** sugar?*

Mwynhau *To enjoy*
*Mae pawb yn **mwynhau**'r cyngerdd yn fawr.*
*Everybody is **enjoying** the concert a lot.*

Mynd *To go*
*Wyt ti'n **mynd** i'r sinema heno?*
*Are you **going** to the cinema tonight?*
*Dw i'n **mynd** i wneud y gwaith cartre heno.*
*I'm **going** to do the homework tonight.*

Mynd am dro *To go for a walk*
*Mi fyddwn ni'n **mynd am dro** i'r parc ar ôl cinio.*
*We will be **going for a walk** in the park after lunch.*

Mynd dros ben llestri *To go over the top, to go too far*
*Dyna ddigon! Dach chi wedi **mynd dros ben llestri**.*
*That's enough! You've **gone over the top** / **gone too far**.*

Mynd â *To take*
*Mi fydd Aled yn **mynd â** chi yn ei gar.*
*Aled will **take** you in his car.*

Mynd â'r ci am dro *To take the dog for a walk*
*Dan ni'n **mynd â'r ci am dro** i'r traeth.*
*We're **taking the dog for a walk** to the beach.*

Mynydd *[eg]* *Mountain*
> mynyddoedd *Dw i'n mynd i ddringo'r **mynydd** fory.*
*I'm going to climb the **mountain** tomorrow.*

N

Nabod *To know [someone or somewhere]*
*Dach chi'n **nabod** fy ngwraig, Mair?*
*Do you **know** my wife, Mair?*
*Dw i wedi bod i'r Rhyl ond dw i ddim yn **nabod** y lle'n dda.*
*I've been to Rhyl but I don't **know** the place well.*

Nadolig, y *[eg]* *Christmas*
Nadolig *llawen a blwyddyn newydd dda i chi!*
*Merry **Christmas** and a happy new year to you!*
*Mae'r **Nadolig** ar 25 Rhagfyr bob blwyddyn.*
***Christmas** is on 25 December every year.*

Nain *[eb]* *Grandmother / Gran / Nan*
> neiniau *Mae fy **nain** yn dŵad o Abergele yn wreiddiol.*
*My **grandmother** comes from Abergele originally.*
*Mi wnaeth **Nain** fynd i weld ei chwaer yn y Fenni.*
***Gran / Nan** went to see her sister in Abergavenny.*

Hen nain   *Great grandmother*
Roedd fy **hen nain** *yn siarad Cymraeg yn dda.*
My **great grandmother** spoke Welsh well.

Neb   *Nobody, no one*
Does 'na **neb** *yn y tŷ ar hyn o bryd.*
There's **nobody** in the house at the moment.

Neges *[eb]*   *Message*
> negeseuon   *Mae hi wedi gadael* **neges** *ar eich peiriant ateb chi.*
She's left a **message** on your answer machine.

Anfon neges   *To send a message*
Mi fydd y tiwtor yn **anfon neges** *am y dosbarth nesa.*
The tutor will be **sending a message** about the next class.

Neges destun *[eb]*   *Text message*
Mi wnes i gael **neges destun** *ar fy ffôn symudol.*
I got a **text message** on my mobile phone.

Neis   *Nice*
Roedd y parti'n **neis** *iawn – mi wnaeth pawb fwynhau.*
The party was very **nice** – everyone enjoyed.

Neithiwr   *Last night*
Neithiwr *mi wnes i fynd i'r dafarn ond heno dw i'n aros adre.*
Last night I went to the pub but tonight I'm staying home.

Nesa   *Next*
Mi fydd y dosbarth **nesa** *ar ôl y Nadolig.*
The **next** class will be after Christmas.

Neu   *Or + Treiglad Meddal*
Be' dach chi'n licio ei yfed: te **neu g**offi? /
> **'ta** *[NW variation] Be' dach chi'n licio ei yfed: te* **'ta** *coffi?*
What do you like drinking: tea **or** coffee?

Neuadd *[eb]*   *Hall*
> neuaddau   *Mi fydd cyngerdd y plant yn y* **neuadd**.
    ***The children's concert will be in the* hall.**

Neuadd y dre   *Town hall*
    Mi wnaeth pawb ddŵad i'r cyfarfod yn **neuadd y dre**.
    Everybody came to the meeting in the town hall.

Neuadd bentre   *Village hall*
    Mae Sadwrn Siarad yn **neuadd bentre** *Aberwylan.*
    There's a Sadwrn Siarad in Aberwylan village hall.

Newid   *To change*
    Fyddwch chi'n **newid** *eich pres cyn y gwyliau?*
    Will you be* changing *your money before the holidays?
    Cyn mynd i'r theatr, mae o'n **newid** *ei ddillad.*
    Before going to the theatre, he* changes *his clothes.

Newyddion *[ell]* *News*
    Mi wnaethon ni gael **newyddion** *da: dan ni wedi ennill car!*
    We had some good* news*: we've won a car!
    Dw i ddim yn licio gwylio'r **newyddion** *ar y teledu.*
    I don't like watching the* news *on the television.

Nhw   *(i) They*
    Maen **nhw**'*n gwrando ar Radio Cymru bob bore.*
    They *listen to Radio Cymru every morning.*
    (ii) Their [+ eu]
    Be' ydy eu cyfeiriad **nhw**?
    What is **their** *address?*

76

Ni

(i) We
*Dan **ni**'n byw yng Nghaerdydd.*
We *live in Cardiff.*
*(ii) our [+ **ein**]*
*Be' ydy ein cyfeiriad **ni**?*
*What is **our** address?*

Niwlog

Misty, foggy
Dw i ddim yn medru gweld llawer: mae hi'n **niwlog** *iawn.*
*I can't see much: it's very **foggy**.*

Nofio

To swim
*Mae Aled yn mynd i **nofio** o Aberystwyth i Bwllheli.*
*Aled is going to **swim** from Aberystwyth to Pwllheli.*

'Nôl

See > Yn ôl

Nos *[eb]*

Night [i.e. as opposed to day or evening.
See also: individual days of the week to say 'Monday night' etc.]
*Dw i ddim yn mynd allan **nos** fory.*
*I'm not going out tomorrow **night**.*

Noson *[eb]*

Night, evening [i.e. over a period of time / the events of the night or evening]
*Roedd neithiwr yn **noson** dda iawn. **Noson** i'w chofio!*
*Last night was a very good **night / evening**. A **night / evening** to remember / to be remembered!*

Noswaith *[eb]*

Evening [i.e. to refer to the time between day and night]
*Croeso i'r cyngerdd a **noswaith** dda i chi i gyd.*
*Welcome to the concert and good **evening** to you all.*

Nunlle
Nowhere / Anywhere [Standard Welsh: Unman]
Dw i ddim yn medru gweld y plant yn nunlle.
I can't see the children anywhere.

Nyrs [eb/eg]
> nyrsys
Nurse
Nyrs *yn Ysbyty Gwynedd ydy Siân.*
Siân's a nurse at Ysbyty Gwynedd.

Nyrsio
To nurse
Ers pryd mae Siân yn nyrsio yn Ysbyty Gwynedd?
Since when / how long has Siân been nursing at Ysbyty Gwynedd?

O

O
Of, from + Treiglad Meddal
Mi wnes i fynd i'r siop i brynu peint o lefrith.
I went to the shop to buy a pint of milk.
Mae Chris yn dŵad o Hirwaun yn wreiddiol.
Chris comes from Hirwaun originally.

O flaen
In front of
Maen nhw wedi gadael eu car o flaen y tŷ.
They have left their car in front of the house.

O gwbl
At all
Popeth yn iawn! Dim problem o gwbl!
Everything's fine! No problem at all!

O gwmpas
Around
Mi fydd y bws yn teithio o gwmpas Cymru.
The bus will be travelling around Wales.

O leia
At least
Mi fydd o leia hanner y dosbarth yn mynd i'r dafarn heno.
At least half the class will be going to the pub tonight.

O'r blaen

Before (hand)
Dw i ddim wedi gweld y bobl yma o'r blaen.
I haven't seen these people **before**.

O'r gloch

O'clock
Mae'r dosbarth yn dechrau am saith o'r gloch.
The class begins at seven **o'clock**.

Oed

Age, [years] old
Maen nhw'n 18 [un deg wyth] oed ac yn
prynu cwrw yn y dafarn am y tro cynta.
They're 18 **years old / aged** 18 and buying
beer in the pub for the first time.
Be' ydy oed eich plant?
How **old** are your children?

Oer

Cold
Fel arfer, mae'n oer iawn ym mis Ionawr.
Usually it's very **cold** in January.

Oeri

To get cold
Roedd hi'n braf iawn heddiw ond mae'n
dechrau oeri rŵan.
It was really lovely today but it's starting to
get cold now.

Ofnadwy

Awful, terrible
Roedd y tywydd yn ofnadwy – roedd hi'n
bwrw glaw bob dydd.
The weather was **terrible / awful** – it was
raining every day.

Ond

But
Mae Eleri'n dŵad i'r parti ond dydy Rachel
ddim yn medru dŵad.
Eleri's coming to the party **but** Rachel can't
come.

Opera sebon *[eb]* *Soap opera*
> operâu sebon **Opera sebon** *ar S4C ydy* Pobol y Cwm.
Pobol y Cwm *is a* **soap opera** *on S4C.*

Oren *Orange*
> orenau *Dw i'n bwyta* **oren** *i frecwast bob bore.*
I eat an **orange** *for breakfast every morning.*
Mae gynnon ni gar **oren**.
We've got an **orange** *(coloured) car.*

Os *If*
Os *dach chi'n barod, i ffwrdd â chi!*
If *you're ready, off you go!*

Os gwelwch yn dda *Please [formal or plural]*
Agorwch y ffenest, **os gwelwch yn dda.**
Open the window, **please.**

Os gweli di'n dda *Please [informal and singular]*
Agora'r ffenest, **os gweli di'n dda.**
Open the window, **please.**

P

Pa? *Which / What?* + *Treiglad Meddal*
Pa ddiwrnod *ydy hi heddiw?*
Which / what *day is it today?*

Pacio *To pack*
Mi fyddwn ni'n **pacio** *ein bagiau ar ddiwedd y gwyliau.*
We will be **packing** *our bags at the end of the holidays.*

Paent *[eg]* *Paint [See also:* **Peintio***]*
Dydy'r **paent** *ddim yn sych eto.*
The **paint***'s not dry yet.*

Peintio   *To paint*
*Mi fyddwn ni'n **peintio**'r stafell yn felyn.*
*We will be **painting** the room yellow.*

Pam?   *Why?*
***Pam** dach chi'n siarad Saesneg efo fi?*
***Why** are you speaking English to me?*

Pan   *When + Treiglad Meddal [use **Pryd?** to ask a question]*
*Dowch i'r tŷ **pan f**yddwch chi'n barod.*
*Come to the house **when** you are (you will be) ready.*

Panad *[eb/eg]* / *A cup of / A cuppa*
*Dan ni'n cael **panad** bob dydd yn y dosbarth.*
*We have a **cuppa** every day in class.*
*Dach chi isio **panad** o de?*
*Do you want a **cup of** tea?*
*[Also used is: **Paned**]*

Papur *[eg]*   *Paper*
> papurau   *Does gen i ddim **papur** ysgrifennu.*
*I haven't got any writing **paper**.*

Papur newydd *[eg] Newspaper*
> papurau newydd *Mae hi'n darllen y **papur newydd** ar ôl brecwast.*
*She reads the **newspaper** after breakfast.*

Pâr *[eg]*   *Pair*
> parau*

Gwaith pâr*   *Work in pairs*

Para*   *To last*
Parc *[eg]*   *Park*
> parciau   *Mi wnes i fynd â'r ci am dro i'r **parc**.*
*I took the dog for a walk to the **park**.*

Parcio	*To park*
	*Maen nhw wedi **parcio**'r car o flaen y siop.*
	They have **parked the car in front of the shop.**
Parod	*Ready*
	*Dach chi'n **barod** i fynd ar y daith?*
	Are you **ready to go on the trip?**
	*[Yn] **barod** pawb?*
	Ready everyone?
Parti *[eg]*	*Party*
> partïon	*Mi fydd y **parti** yn y neuadd am chwech o'r gloch.*
	The **party will be in the hall at six o'clock.**

Parti pen-blwydd *[eg]* Birthday party
*Dw i'n rhy hen i gael **parti pen-blwydd**!*
I'm too old to have a **birthday party!**

Partner *[eg]*	*Partner*
> partneriaid	*Gweithiwch efo'ch **partner** am bum munud.*
	Work with your **partner for five minutes.**
	*Dowch â ffrind neu **bartner** i'r parti.*
	Bring a friend or **partner to the party.**
Pasg, y *[eg]*	*Easter*
	*Does 'na ddim ysgol dros y **Pasg**.*
	There's no school over **Easter.**
Pasta *[eg]*	*Pasta*
	*Maen nhw'n bwyta **pasta** yn yr Eidal.*
	They eat **pasta in Italy.**
Pawb	*Everybody, everyone*
	*Ydy **pawb** yn medru dŵad i'r dosbarth wythnos nesa?*
	Can **everyone / everybody come to the class next week?**
	*Da iawn **pawb** – unwaith eto!!*
	Well done **everyone – once again!!**

Peidio (â)   *To not do something*
Peidiwch â siarad Saesneg yn y dosbarth!
Don't / Do not *speak English in class!*

Peint *[eg]*   *Pint*
Mi fydda i'n cael **peint** *(o gwrw) yn y dafarn heno.*
I'll be having a **pint** *(of beer) in the pub tonight.*

Peiriant *[eg]*   *Machine*
> peiriannau   *Dydy'r* **peiriant** *ddim yn gweithio: mae o wedi torri.*
The **machine** *isn't working: it's broken.*

Peiriant ateb   *Answer machine / phone*
Gadewch neges ar y **peiriant** *ateb.*
Leave a message on the **answer machine**.

Peiriant CD   *CD machine*
Gwrandewch ar y canu ar y **peiriant CD**.
Listen to the singing on the **CD machine**.

Peiriant DVD   *DVD machine*
Gwyliwch y ffilm ar y **peiriant DVD**.
Watch the film on the **DVD machine**.

Peiriant golchi   *Washing machine*
Rhowch eich dillad yn y **peiriant golchi**.
Put your clothes in the **washing machine**.

Peiriant golchi llestri *[eg]*   *Dishwasher*
Ar ôl bwyd, rhowch bopeth yn y **peiriant golchi llestri**.
After food, put everything in the **dishwasher**.

Pêl *[eb]*   *Ball*
> peli   *Mae'r* **bêl** *wedi mynd i ardd drws nesa.*
The **ball** *has gone into next door's garden.*

Pêl-droed *[eg]*   *Football*

Roedd y plant yn chwarae **pêl-droed** *ar y stryd.*

The children were playing football on the street.

Pell   *Far*

Mae America'n **bell** *o Gymru.*

America is far from Wales.

Pen *[eg]*   *Head*

> pennau   *Gwisgwch het i gadw eich* **pen** *yn sych.*

Wear a hat to keep your head dry.

Pen-blwydd *[eg]*   *Birthday*

21 [dau ddeg un] oed heddiw? **Pen-blwydd** *hapus i ti!*

21 today? Happy birthday to you!

Pennaeth *[eg]*   *Head [Also in school context:* **Prifathro / Prifathrawes** *– Headmaster / Headmistress]*

Mae'r **pennaeth** *newydd isio newid popeth yn yr ysgol.*

The new head wants to change everything in the school.

Pensil *[eg]*   *Pencil*

> pensiliau   *Mae gynni hi* **bensil** *ac mae hi'n barod i ysgrifennu.*

She's got a pencil and she's ready to write.

Pentre *[eg]*   *Village*

> pentrefi   *Dan ni'n byw mewn* **pentre** *bach yn y wlad.*

We live in a small village in the country.

Penwythnos *[eg]* *Weekend*

> penwythnosau *Fydda i ddim yn gweithio dros y* **penwythnos**.

I won't be working over the weekend.

Person *[eg]*   *Person*

> pobl / personau *Dach chi'n nabod y* **person** *newydd yn y dosbarth?*

Do you know the new person in class?

Peswch [eg]   Cough
Mae o'n smygu gormod ac mae gynno fo
beswch *rŵan.*
*He smokes too much and he's got a **cough** now.*

Peth [eg]   Thing
> pethau   *Be' ydy enw'r **peth** yna yn Gymraeg?*
*What's the name of that **thing** in Welsh?*
*Dyna'r **peth** pwysig.*
*That's the **important** thing.*

Plentyn [eg]   Child
> plant   *Fel **plentyn**, ro'n i'n mynd i ysgol Gymraeg.*
*As a **child**, I went to a Welsh medium-school.*
*Mae gen i bedwar **plentyn** / Mae gen i*
*bedwar o **blant**.*
*I've got four **children**.*

Plismon [eg]   Policeman
> plismyn
Plismones [eb]   Policewoman
> plismonesau   **Plismon** *ydy Marc – mae o'n gweithio efo*
Heddlu Gwent.
*Marc is a **policeman** – he works with Gwent*
Police.
Plismones *ydy Elen – mae hi'n gweithio efo*
Heddlu Gogledd Cymru.
*Elen is a **policewoman** – she works with*
North Wales Police.

Pob   Each, every
*Erbyn hyn, mae **pob** dysgwr yn siarad*
Cymraeg yn gynta.
*By now, **every** learner speaks Welsh first.*

Pob un   Each / Every one
*Mi fydd **pob un** o'r plant yn canu yn y cyngerdd.*
Every / each one of the children will be singing in the
concert.

Pobl [eb]
People
*Mae **pobl** yn gyrru ar y dde yn Ffrainc.*
People drive on the right in France.

Poeni
To worry
*Peidiwch â **phoeni**! Mi fydd popeth yn iawn.*
Don't **worry**! Everything will be OK.

Poeth
Hot
*Yn Sbaen, mae hi'n **boeth** iawn ym mis Awst.*
In Spain, it's very **hot** in August.

Pont [eb]
> pontydd
Bridge
*Mi wnaethon ni yrru dros **Bont** Hafren, o Gymru i Loegr.*
We drove over the Severn **Bridge**, from Wales to England.

Popeth
Everything
*Erbyn hyn, dw i'n dallt **popeth** yn y dosbarth.*
By now, I understand **everything** in class.
***Popeth** yn iawn!*
Everything's OK / fine!

Porc [eg]
Pork
*Mi wnaethon ni gael **porc** i ginio dydd Sul.*
We had **pork** for Sunday lunch.

Post [eg]
Post
*Mae'r llythyr yn y **post**.*
The letter's in the **post**.

Postio
To post
*Mi wnes i **bostio**'r llythyr ddoe.*
I **posted** the letter yesterday.

Postmon [eg]
> postmyn
Postman / woman
*Mi fydd y **postmon** yn dŵad â'r llythyr fory.*
The **postman** will be bringing the letter tomorrow.

Potel [eb]
> poteli
Bottle
*Mae hi'n yfed **potel** o lefrith bob dydd.*
She drinks a **bottle** of milk every day.

Pres *[eg]*   *Money [Standard Welsh: **Arian**]*
                   Dw i ddim yn medru talu – does gen i ddim
                   pres.
                   *I can't pay – I haven't got any **money**.*

Pres cinio   *Dinner money*
                   *Mae'r athro'n gofyn am y **pres cinio** bob bore Llun.*
                   *The teacher asks for **dinner money** every Monday.*

Pres poced   *Pocket money*
                   *Dydy Siôn ddim yn cael llawer o **bres poced**, felly mae*
                   o'n gweithio mewn caffi ar y penwythnos.
                   *Siôn doesn't get much **pocket money**, so he works in a*
                   café at the weekend.

Priod, yn briod *Married*
                   *Mae Liz a Richard **yn briod** ers blwyddyn*
                   rŵan.
                   *Liz and Richard have been **married** for a*
                   year now.

Pris *[eg]*   *Price*
> prisiau   *Be' ydy **pris** y tocyn?*
                   *What's the **price** of the ticket?*

Problem *[eb]* *Problem*
> problemau   *Dim **problem** o gwbl!*
                   *No **problem** at all!*

Pryd?   *When [to ask a question]?*
                   ***Pryd** mae'r ddrama'n dechrau?*
                   ***When** is the play starting?*

Prynu   *To buy*
                   *Dach chi wedi **prynu** eich anrhegion Nadolig*
                   eto?
                   *Have you **bought** your Christmas presents*
                   yet?

Prysur *Busy*
Mae'r siopau'n **brysur** *iawn dros y Nadolig.*
The shops are very **busy** *over Christmas.*

Punt *[eb]* *Pound [£]*
> punnoedd / punnau *Pris y llyfr ydy pum* **punt**.
The price of the book is five **pounds**.

Pupur *[eg]* *Pepper*
Roedd y **pupur** *yn boeth iawn.*
The **pepper** *was very hot.*
Pupur *a halen.*
Pepper *and salt.*

Pwdin *[eg]* *Pudding*
> pwdinau *Does 'na neb isio* **pwdin** *ar ôl cinio.*
Nobody wants **pudding** *after lunch.*

Pwll nofio *[eg]* *Swimming pool*
> pyllau nofio *Oes 'na* **bwll nofio** *yn y ganolfan hamdden?*
Is there a **swimming pool** *in the leisure centre?*

Pwy? *Who?*
Pwy *dach chi?*
Who *are you?*
Pwy *ydy tiwtor y dosbarth?*
Who *is the class tutor?*
Pwy *sy'n dŵad i'r dafarn efo chi?*
Who *is coming to the pub with you?*

Pwysig *Important*
Mae'n **bwysig** *siarad Cymraeg bob tro.*
It's **important** *to speak Welsh every time.*

Pys *[ell]* *Peas*
Dw i'n licio bwyta porc, **pys** *a sglodion.*
I like eating pork, **peas** *and chips.*

Pysgodyn *[eg]* *Fish*
> pysgod *Enw'r* **pysgodyn** *ydy Nemo.*
The **fish** *is called Nemo.*

Mae 'na ddigon o **bysgod** *yn y môr.*
There are enough / plenty of **fish** *in the sea.*

Pysgodyn aur *Goldfish*
Dw i wedi ennill **pysgodyn aur***!*
I've won a **goldfish***!*

R

Radio *[eg]* *Radio*
Dw i'n gwrando ar y **radio** *yn y car.*
I listen to the **radio** *in the car.*

Rŵan *Now*
Dw i yn y dosbarth **rŵan** *– wedyn mi fydda i'n mynd adre.*
I'm in class **now** *– then I'll be going home.*

Rygbi *[eg]* *Rugby*
Roedd Gareth yn chwarae **rygbi** *yn y parc ddoe.*
Gareth was playing **rugby** *in the park yesterday.*

RH

Rhagfyr *[mis]* *December*
Mis rhif un deg dau ydy mis **Rhagfyr***.*
December *is month number twelve.*

Rhaglen *[eb]* *Programme*
> rhaglenni *Roedd enwau'r actorion yn y* **rhaglen***.*
The names of the actors were in the **programme***.*
Dan ni'n mwynhau'r **rhaglenni** *ar S4C.*
We enjoy the **programmes** *on S4C.*

Rhaid *[eg]*　　*Necessity > used to say you 'must´ do something*
Rhaid i bawb siarad Cymraeg yn y dosbarth.
*Everyone **must** speak Welsh in class.*

Rhain (y)　　*These*
*Fy llyfrau i ydy'r **rhain**.*
***These** are my books.*

Rheina (y)　　*Those*
*Dy lyfrau di ydy'r **rheina**.*
***Those** are your books.*

Rhedeg　　*To run*
*Roedd Guto Nyth Brân yn medru **rhedeg** yn gyflym iawn.*
*Guto Nyth Brân could **run** very quickly.*

Rhiant *[eg]*　　*Parent/s*
> rhieni
*Mae croeso i bob **rhiant** yn yr ysgol newydd.*
*Every **parent** is welcome in the new school.*
*Mi fydd 'na noson **rieni** yn yr ysgol heno.*
*There will be a **parents'** evening in the school tonight.*

Rhif *[eg]*　　*Number [= numeral]*
> rhifau
*Dw i wedi ennill y bingo! Dyma fy **rhifau** i.*
*I've won the bingo! Here are my **numbers**.*

Rhoi　　*(i) To give*
*Wyt ti wedi **rhoi**'r anrheg ben-blwydd i Siân?*
*Have you **given** Siân the birthday present / **given** the birthday present to Siân?*
(ii) To put
*Maen nhw'n **rhoi**'r pres ar y bwrdd.*
*They **put** the money on the table.*

Rhwng　　*Between*
*Mae Llandudno **rhwng** Bangor a Wrecsam.*
*Llandudno is **between** Bangor and Wrexham.*

Rhy	*Too* + *Treiglad Meddal*
	Dw i ddim yn medru yfed y te yma. Mae'n **rhy b**oeth.
	I can't drink this tea. It's **too** *hot.*
Rhywbeth	*Something*
	Roedd 'na **rywbeth** *i bawb yn y sioe.*
	There was **something** *for everyone in the show.*
Rhywun	*Someone / Somebody*
	Mae 'na **rywun** *wrth y drws – pwy?*
	There's **someone** *at the door – who?*

S

Sadwrn, dydd	*Saturday*
	Dw i'n mynd i wylio rygbi bob **dydd Sadwrn**.
	I go to watch rugby every **Saturday**.
Nos Sadwrn	*Saturday night*
	Maen nhw'n mynd allan i'r dre **nos Sadwrn**.
	They are going out to town on **Saturday night**.
Sadwrn Siarad	*A Saturday all-day course with emphasis on speaking Welsh*
Saesneg	*(i) English (language)* [adjective]
	Rhaglen **Saesneg** *ydy* Coronation Street.
	Coronation Street *is an* **English (language)** *programme.*
	(ii) English language [noun]
	Does 'na neb yn siarad **Saesneg** *yn y dosbarth.*
	Nobody speaks **English** *in class.*
Sais [eg]	*An Englishman*
Saesnes [eb]	*An English woman*
> Saeson	*The English*

Sais ydy Reginald – mae o'n dŵad o Leeds yn wreiddiol.

Reginald is **English** *(i.e. an Englishman) – he comes from Leeds originally.*

Saesnes ydy Pippa – mae hi'n dŵad o Windsor yn wreiddiol.

Pippa is **English** *(i.e. an English woman) – she comes from Windsor originally.*

Sâl — *Ill*

Dydy hi ddim yn y gwaith heddiw – mae hi'n **sâl**.

She's not in work today – she's **ill**.

Salad *[eg]* — *Salad*
> saladau

Dan ni'n licio bwyta **salad** yn yr haf.

We like eating **salad** *in the summer.*

Sbaen *[eb]* — *Spain*

Mae Madrid a Málaga yn **Sbaen**.

Madrid and Málaga are in **Spain**.

Sbectol *[eb]* — *Glasses*

Rhaid i mi wisgo **sbectol** i ddarllen.

I have to wear **glasses** *to read.*

Sgio — *To ski, go skiing*

Dan ni'n mynd i **sgio** yn Aviemore ym mis Chwefror.

We're **going skiing** *in Aviemore in February.*

Sglodion *[ell]* — *Chips*

Maen nhw'n bwyta **sglodion** efo popeth!

They eat **chips** *with everything!*

Sgrifennu — *See >* **Ysgrifennu**

Sgwennu — *See >* **Ysgrifennu**

Sgwrs *[eb]* — *Chat, conversation*
> sgyrsiau

Dw i'n mwynhau **sgwrs** fach yn Gymraeg.

I enjoy a little **chat** *in Welsh.*

Siaced *[eb]* *Jacket*
> siacedi *Mae Siôn wedi gadael ei **siaced** yn y dafarn.*
*Siôn has left his **jacket** in the pub.*

Siarad (efo) *To speak, talk (to)*
*Dach chi'n **siarad** Cymraeg?*
*Do you **speak** Welsh?*
*Dw i'n **siarad** Cymraeg **efo** nhw bob tro.*
*I always **talk to** them in Welsh.*

Sigarét *[eb]* *Cigarette*
> sigaréts *Maen nhw o flaen y dafarn yn smygu **sigarét**.*
They are in front of the pub smoking a
***cigarette**.*

Sillafu *To spell*
*Sut dach chi'n **sillafu**'r gair 'cyfarwyddiadau'?*
*How do you **spell** the word 'cyfarwyddiadau'?*

Sinema *[eb]* *Cinema*
> sinemâu *Pa ffilm wnaethoch chi ei gweld yn y*
***sinema** neithiwr?*
*Which film did you see in the **cinema** last*
night?

Siocled *[eg]* *Chocolate*
> siocledi *Ar ôl bwyta gormod o **siocled**, roedd hi'n sâl.*
*After eating too much **chocolate**, she was ill.*

Siocled twym / poeth *Hot chocolate*
*Cyn mynd i'r gwely, dw i'n yfed **siocled poeth**.*
*Before going to bed, I drink **hot chocolate**.*

Sioe *[eb]* *Show*
> sioeau *Mi fydd 'na lawer o bobl enwog yn y **sioe***
eleni.
There will be many famous people in the
***show** this year.*

Siôn Corn *[eg]*   *Father Christmas*
Mae **Siôn Corn** *yn galw bob Nadolig.*
Father Christmas *calls every Christmas.*

Siop *[eb]*   *Shop*
> siopau
Dydy'r **siop** *ddim yn agor ddydd Sul.*
The **shop** *doesn't open on Sunday.*

Siop bapurau   *Paper shop / Newsagents*
Maen nhw'n gwerthu papurau yn y **siop bapurau.**
They sell papers in the **newsagents / paper shop.**

Siop ddillad   *Clothes shop*
Maen nhw'n gwerthu dillad yn y **siop ddillad.**
They sell clothes in the **clothes shop.**

Siop fara   *Bread shop / Baker's*
Maen nhw'n gwerthu bara yn y **siop fara.**
They sell bread in the **baker's / bread shop.**

Siop fwyd   *Food shop*
Maen nhw'n gwerthu bwyd yn y **siop fwyd.**
They sell food in the **food shop.**

Siop lyfrau   *Book shop*
Maen nhw'n gwerthu llyfrau yn y **siop lyfrau.**
They sell books in the **book shop.**

Siop sglodion   *Chip shop*
Maen nhw'n gwerthu sglodion yn y **siop sglodion.**
They sell chips in the **chip shop.**

Siopa   *To shop*
Dan ni'n **siopa** *am fwyd unwaith yr wythnos.*
We **shop** *for food once a week.*

Siopwr *[eg]*   *(i) Shopper*
> siopwyr
Roedd 'na lawer o **siopwyr** *yn y dre cyn y Nadolig.*
There were many **shoppers** *in town before Christmas.*

(ii) Shopkeeper
*Mi wnaeth y **siopwr** brynu'r siop yn 2012.*
The shopkeeper bought the shop in 2012.

Siwgr *[eg]*
Sugar
*Dw i ddim yn licio **siwgr** mewn coffi.*
I don't like sugar in coffee.

Siŵr
Sure, certain
*Dan ni ddim yn **siŵr** pryd bydd o'n cyrraedd.*
We aren't sure when he'll be arriving.

Siŵr o fod
Probably
*Mi fydd o'n cyrraedd yn hwyr, **siŵr o fod**.*
*He will **probably** be arriving late.*

Smwddio
To iron, do the ironing
*Rhaid i chi **smwddio** eich dillad cyn mynd allan.*
You must iron your clothes before going out.

Smygu
To smoke
*Does 'na ddim **smygu** yn y tafarnau yng Nghymru.*
There's no smoking in the pubs in Wales.

Stadiwm *[eg]*
Stadium
*Mi fyddan nhw'n chwarae yn y **stadiwm** newydd.*
They will be playing in the new stadium.

Stafell *[eb]*
> stafelloedd
Room [in a building]
*Mae'r dosbarth mewn **stafell** fawr.*
The class is in a big room.

Stafell fwyta
> stafelloedd bwyta
Dining room
*Mi fydd swper yn y **stafell fwyta**.*
*Dinner will be in the **dining room**.*

Stafell fyw
> stafelloedd byw
Living room
*Dan ni'n edrych ar y teledu yn y **stafell fyw**.*
*We watch television in the **living room**.*

Stafell wely — *Bedroom*
> stafelloedd gwely — *Maen nhw isio prynu tŷ efo pedair **stafell wely**.*
*They want to buy a house with four **bedrooms**.*

Stafell ymolchi — *Bathroom*
> stafelloedd ymolchi — *Dw i'n mynd i gael bath yn y **stafell ymolchi**.*
*I'm going to have a bath in the **bathroom**.*

Stopio — *To stop*
*Dyna ddigon – **stopiwch** rŵan!*
*That's enough – **stop** now!*

Stori *[eb]* — *Story*
> straeon — *Does 'na ddim digon o amser rŵan – mae hi'n **stori** hir.*

occ. straeon — *There's not enough time now – it's a long **story**.*

*Roedd y plant yn mwynhau amser **stori**.*
*The children used to enjoy **story** time.*

Stormus — *Stormy*
*Mi fydd hi'n noson **stormus** heno, efo llawer o wynt a glaw.*
*It'll be a **stormy** night tonight, with a lot of wind and rain.*

Stryd *[eb]* — *Street*
> strydoedd — *Does 'na neb arall yn byw yn ein **stryd** ni.*
*Nobody else lives in our **street**.*

Stryd fawr — *High street*
*Mae llawer o siopau'r **stryd fawr** wedi cau.*
*Many of the **high street** shops have closed.*

Sudd *[eg]* — *Juice*
*Dw i'n yfed **sudd** oren / afal i frecwast.*
*I drink orange / apple **juice** for breakfast.*

Sul, dydd *Sunday*
*Dw i byth yn gweithio ar **ddydd Sul**.*
*I never work on **Sunday(s)**.*

Nos Sul *Sunday night*
*Maen nhw'n mynd i'r gwely'n gynnar ar **nos Sul**.*
*They go to bed early on **Sunday night(s)**.*

Sut? *How?*
Sut *dach chi?*
How *are you?*
Sut *dach chi'n deud 'how' yn Gymraeg?*
How *do you say 'how' in Welsh?*

Swper *[eg]* *Supper*
> swperau *Am faint o'r gloch mae **swper** heno?*
*What time is **supper** tonight?*

Swyddfa *[eb]* *Office*
> swyddfeydd *Dan ni'n gweithio mewn **swyddfa** yng*
nghanol y dre.
*We work in an **office** in the centre of town.*

Swyddfa bost *Post office*
> swyddfeydd post *Mae hi wedi mynd i'r **swyddfa bost** i bostio llythyr.*
*She has gone to the **post office** to post a letter.*

Sych *Dry*
*Fory, mi fydd hi'n braf ac yn **sych**.*
*Tomorrow, it will be fine and **dry**.*

Syched *Thirsty [lit: 'thirst'] [Standard Welsh]*
See > **Isio diod**

Symud *To move*
*Mae'r dosbarth wedi **symud** o'r neuadd i'r ysgol.*
*The class has **moved** from the hall to the school.*

Symud (tŷ) *To move (house)*
*Mi wnaethon ni **symud** o Aberystwyth i Gaerfyrddin.*
*We **moved** from Aberystwyth to Carmarthen.*

Syniad *[eg]*　　*Idea*
> syniadau　　*Mae o'n **syniad** da.*
　　　　　　　　*It's a good **idea**.*
　　　　　　　　*Does gen i ddim **syniad**.*
　　　　　　　　*I have no **idea**.*
Syth　　　　*Straight*
　　　　　　　　*Mi fydda i'n mynd yn **syth** i'r dosbarth heno.*
　　　　　　　　*I will be going **straight** to class tonight.*

Syth ymlaen　　*Straight on [directions]*
　　　　　　　　*Trowch i'r dde, yna ewch yn **syth ymlaen**.*
　　　　　　　　*Turn to the right, then go **straight on**.*

T

Tabled *[eb]*　　*Tablet*
> tabledi　　*Os oes gynnoch chi gur pen, rhaid i chi gymryd **tabled**.*
　　　　　　　　*If you've got a headache, you must take a **tablet**.*
Tacsi *[eg]*　　*Taxi*
> tacsis　　*Mi wnes i fynd adre o'r dafarn mewn **tacsi**.*
　　　　　　　　*I went home from the pub in a **taxi**.*
Tachwedd *[mis]* *November*
　　　　　　　　*Mis rhif un deg un ydy mis **Tachwedd**.*
　　　　　　　　***November** is month number eleven.*
Tad *[eg]* / **Dad** / **Dadi**　　*Father / Dad / Daddy*
> tadau　　*Mae **tad** Ffion yn byw yng Nglyn Ebwy.*
　　　　　　　　*Ffion's **father** lives in Ebbw Vale.*
　　　　　　　　*Mi wnaeth **Dad** fynd i weld ei ffrind yng Nghaergybi.*
　　　　　　　　***Dad** went to see his friend in Holyhead.*

Tad yng nghyfraith *Father-in-law*
　　　　　　　　*Enw fy **nhad yng nghyfraith** (tad fy ngŵr) ydy Gareth.*
　　　　　　　　*My **father-in-law** (my husband's father)'s name is Gareth.*

Tafarn [eb]
> tafarnau

Pub, tavern
Dach chi isio dŵad i'r **dafarn** *efo ni?*
Do you want to come to the pub with us?

Taflen [eb]
> taflenni

Leaflet, handout, sheet
Ysgrifennwch yr atebion ar y **daflen**.
Write the answers on the sheet.

Taflen waith

Worksheet
> taflenni gwaith
Gwnewch y **daflen waith** *erbyn yr wythnos nesa.*
Do the worksheet by next week.

Taid [eg]
> teidiau

Grandfather / Grandpa / Grampy
Mae fy **nhaid** *yn dŵad o Abergwaun yn wreiddiol.*
My grandfather comes from Fishguard originally.
Mi wnaeth **Taid** *fynd i weld ei chwaer ym Mhrestatyn.*
Grandpa / Grampy went to see his sister in Prestatyn.

Hen daid

Great grandfather
Roedd fy **hen daid** *yn siarad Cymraeg yn dda.*
My great grandfather spoke Welsh well.

Taith [eb]
> teithiau

Trip, journey [See also: **Teithio**]
Mae'r **daith** *o Abertawe i Fangor yn hir.*
The journey / trip from Swansea to Bangor is long.

Tal

Tall
Mae Ifan yn **dal**.
Ifan is **tall**.

Talu + am

To pay (a bill etc) + for
Dach chi wedi **talu** *am y bwyd eto?*
Have you paid for the food yet?

Tan
Until + Treiglad Meddal
*Mi fyddwn ni'n aros **tan dd**ydd Llun nesa.*
*We will be staying **until** next Monday.*

Tân *[eg]*
> tanau
Fire
*Mi wnaethon ni eistedd o flaen y **tân** yn y dafarn.*
*We sat in front of the **fire** in the pub.*

Ar dân
On fire
*Rhedwch! Mae'r tŷ **ar dân**!*
*Run! The house is **on fire**!*

Tatws *[ell]*
Potatoes
*Maen nhw'n gwneud sglodion o'r **tatws**.*
*They're making chips from the **potatoes**.*

Te *[eg]*
Tea (i) drink
*Dw i'n yfed paned o **de** bob bore.*
*I drink a cup of **tea** every morning.*
Tea (ii) mealtime
*Be' sy i **de** heno?*
*What's for **tea** tonight?*

Tedi *[eg]*
> tedis
Teddy
*Mi wnaeth y plentyn fynd â'r **tedi** i'r ysgol.*
*The child took the **teddy** to school.*

Tegan *[eg]*
> teganau
Toy
*Mae'r plant yn chwarae efo eu **teganau**.*
*The children are playing with their **toys**.*

Teimlo
To feel
*Dw i ddim yn **teimlo**'n dda – dw i'n mynd adre.*
*I don't **feel** well – I'm going home.*

Teisen *[eb]*
> teisennau
Cake
*Mi wnaethon ni brynu **teisen** siocled fawr ar ei pen-blwydd hi.*
*We bought a big chocolate **cake** on her birthday.*
*[See also: **Cacen**]*

Teithio
To travel
*Mi fydda i'n **teithio** i Ffrainc fory.*
*I'll be **travelling** to France tomorrow.*

Teledu *[eg]*
Television, TV
*Be' sy ar y **teledu** heno?*
*What's on **television / TV** tonight?*

Tennis *[eg]*
Tennis
*Dan ni'n chwarae **tennis** yn y ganolfan hamdden.*
*We play **tennis** in the leisure centre.*

Teulu *[eg]*
> teuluoedd
Family
*Mae gynnon ni **deulu** mawr.*
*We have a large **family**.*
*Oes gynnoch chi **deulu** yng Nghymru?*
*Do you have **family** in Wales?*

Ti / di
(i) You [informal singular]
*Helo, Aled. Sut wyt **ti** heddiw?*
*Hello, Aled. How are **you** today?*
*Siwan, wyt **ti**'n barod?*
*Siwan, are **you** ready?*
*(ii) Your [+ **dy**]*
*Ydy dy blant **di**'n mynd i ysgol Gymraeg?*
*Do **your** children go to a Welsh-medium school?*

Tîm *[eg]*
> timau
Team
*Dw i'n chwarae yn y **tîm** pêl-droed.*
*I play in the football **team**.*

Tipyn [o]
A bit [of], a little
*Mae Glasgow yn bell. Mae 'na **dipyn** o ffordd i fynd eto!*
*Glasgow's far. There's a **bit of** a way to go yet!*

Tipyn bach
A little bit
*Paned o de a **thipyn bach** o lefrith, os gwelwch yn dda.*
*A cup of tea and **a little bit (drop)** of milk please.*

Tiwtor *[eg]*
> tiwtoriaid

Tutor
*Mae'r **tiwtor** yma'n dysgu'r dosbarth nos Lun.*
This tutor teaches the class on Monday night.

Tocyn *[eg]*
> tocynnau

Ticket
*Dan ni'n mynd i brynu **tocyn** i'r gêm.*
We're going to buy a **ticket** for the game.

Torri

To break
*Ydy'r ffenest wedi **torri**?*
Has the window **broken**?
*Mae'r car wedi **torri** i lawr.*
The car has **broken** down.

Tost *[eg]*

Toast
*Dw i'n licio bwyta **tost** a jam i frecwast.*
I like eating **toast** and jam for breakfast.

Traeth *[eg]*
> traethau

Beach
*Yn yr haf, dan ni'n mynd i'r **traeth** bob dydd.*
In the summer, we go to the **beach** every day.

Tre *[eb]*
> trefi

Town
***Tre** fach hyfryd ydy Dinbych.*
Denbigh's a lovely little **town**.

Treiglad*

Mutation

Treiglad Meddal*	*Soft Mutation*
Treiglad Llaes*	*Aspirate Mutation*
Treiglad Trwynol*	*Nasal Mutation*

Trên *[eg]*
> trenau

Train
*Mi fydd y **trên** nesa yn gadael am un o'r gloch.*
The next **train** will be leaving at one o'clock.

Trist

Sad
*Mi wnaethon ni gael newyddion **trist** y bore yma.*
We had some **sad** news this morning.

Tro *[eg]*
> troeon

*Turn [See also: **Mynd** > **Mynd am dro**]*
*Eich **tro** chi ydy hi rŵan.*
It's your turn now.

Bob tro

Every time
Bob tro *dw i'n gweld Siân, mae hi'n siarad Cymraeg efo fi.*
Every time *I see Siân, she speaks Welsh to me.*

Troed *[eb]*
> traed

Foot
*Rhowch eich **troed** yn y dŵr!*
Put your foot in the water!

Troi

To turn
*Dach chi'n **troi** i'r dde ar ôl y capel.*
You turn to the right after the chapel.
***Trowch** i dudalen 10 [deg], os gwelwch yn dda!*
Turn to page 10, please!

Trwy

Through + Treiglad Meddal
*Mi fydda i'n gyrru **trwy g**anol y dre.*
I will be driving through the centre of town.
*Anfonwch y siec **trwy**'r post!*
Send the cheque through the post!

Trwy'r amser

All the time
*Maen nhw'n siarad Cymraeg efo ni **trwy'r amser**.*
*They speak Welsh to us **all the time**.*

Trwyn *[eg]*
> trwynau

Nose
*Mae gynno fo **drwyn** hir.*
He's got a long nose.

Tu ôl i

Behind
*Mae 'na faes parcio mawr **tu ôl i**'r siop.*
There's a big car park behind the shop.

Tudalen *[eb]*
> tudalennau

Page
Roedd 'na air Cymraeg newydd ar bob **tudalen**.
There was a new Welsh word on every **page**.

Tŷ *[eg]*
> tai

House
Dan ni'n byw mewn **tŷ** *hyfryd yn y wlad.*
We live in a lovely **house** *in the country.*

Tŷ bach *[eg]*
> tai bach

Toilet [Also: **Toiled(au)** *and in NW:* **Lle chwech***]*
Lle mae'r **tŷ bach** */* **lle chwech***, os gwelwch yn dda?*
Where's the **toilet** *please?*

Tywydd *[eg]*

Weather
Sut mae'r **tywydd** *heddiw?*
How's the **weather** *today? / What's the* **weather** *like today?*

TH

Theatr *[eb]*
> theatrau

Theatre
Mae'r actor yn gweithio mewn **theatr**.
The actor works in a **theatre**.

U

Uned *[eb]*
> unedau

Unit
Heno, mi fyddwn ni'n edrych ar **uned** *newydd.*
Tonight, we will be looking at a new **unit**.

Unigol*

Singular

Unman

Nowhere / Anywhere [Standard Welsh]
See > **Nunlle**

Unwaith (eto)	*Once (again)*
	Da iawn! Unwaith eto, os gwelwch yn dda!
	*Well done! **Once again**, please!*
Ar unwaith	*Immediately, straight away*
	*Dowch i'r ysgol **ar unwaith**.*
	*Come to school **immediately**.*

W

Wal *[eb]*	*Wall*
> waliau	*Mi fydda i'n rhoi'r llun ar y **wal**.*
	*I will be putting the picture on the **wall**.*
Wedi	*(i) Past*
	*Mae'n bum munud **wedi** saith.*
	*It's five minutes **past** seven.*
	(ii) Way of making the perfect tense in
	*Welsh e.g. **has** gone rather than **is** going.*
	*Dach chi **wedi** bwyta eto?*
	***Have** you **eaten** yet?*
Wedyn	*(i) After(wards)*
	*Mi fydda i'n eich gweld chi **wedyn**.*
	*I'll be seeing you **after(wards)**.*
	(ii) Then (i.e. what happened next)
	***Wedyn**, mi wnaeth pawb fynd i'r dafarn.*
	***Then**, everyone went to the pub.*
Weithiau	*Sometimes*
	***Weithiau**, dw i'n anghofio ei enw fo.*
	***Sometimes**, I forget his name.*
Wrth	*By / At / Beside [See also: **Deud wrth**] +*
	Treiglad Meddal
	*Pwy sy **wrth** y drws?*
	*Who's **at** the door?*
	*Maen nhw'n byw i lawr **wrth d**afarn y pentre.*
	*They live down **by** the village pub.*

Wrth gwrs	*Of course*
	Dach chi'n siarad Cymraeg? **Wrth gwrs**!
	Do you speak Welsh? **Of course**!
Wrth ymyl	*Close, near*
	Mae Stadiwm y Mileniwm **wrth ymyl** *canol Caerdydd.*
	The Millennium Stadium is **near** *the centre of Cardiff.*
	[See also: **Agos**]
Wy *[eg]*	*Egg*
> wyau	*Dan ni'n cael* **wy** *a sglodion i de eto heno!*
	We're having **egg** *and chips for tea again tonight!*
Wythnos *[eb]*	*Week*
> wythnosau	*Mi fydd y dosbarth yn dechrau yr* **wythnos** *nesa.*
	The class will be starting next **week**.

Y

Y / Yr / 'r	*The*
	Dw i'n gweld **y** *car.*
	I see **the** *car.*
	*Dw i'n gyrru'***r** *car.*
	I drive **the** *car.*
	Car **yr** *heddlu ydy o.*
	It's **the** *police car – it's* **the** *car of the police.*
Yfed	*To drink*
	Dan ni ddim yn gyrru ar ôl **yfed**.
	We don't drive after **drinking**.
Yfory	*See >* **Fory**
Yma	*Here*
	Ydy Siân **yma**?
	Is Siân here?

Ymarfer*	*To practise*
Ymddeol	*To retire [> **wedi ymddeol** = retired]*
	*Mi fydda i'n **ymddeol** y flwyddyn nesa.*
	*I will be **retiring** next year.*
	*Mae Jac **wedi ymddeol** yn barod.*
	*Jac has already **retired**.*
Ymlacio	*To relax*
	*Dw i'n licio **ymlacio** yn y bath ar ôl y dosbarth.*
	*I like to **relax** in the bath after class.*
Ymlaen	*(i) On*
	*Mae'r teledu **ymlaen** trwy'r amser.*
	*The television is **on** all the time.*
	(ii) Ahead, forward
	*Dw i'n mynd i symud **ymlaen** i'r cwrs Sylfaen.*
	*I'm going to move **on / forward / ahead** to the Sylfaen course.*
Ymolchi	*To wash (yourself), to have a wash*
	*Bob bore, dw i'n codi ac yn **ymolchi** cyn gwisgo.*
	*Every morning, I get up and **have a wash** before getting dressed.*
Yn	*Not translated in English but used:*
	(i) with a verb-noun
	*Mae Siân **yn** siarad Cymraeg.*
	*Siân **speaks / is speaking** Welsh: yn + siarad.*
	(ii) with an adjective + Treiglad Meddal
	*Mae'r car **yn g**och.*
	*The car is **red**: yn + coch.*
	(iii) with an adverb + Treiglad Meddal
	*Mae Llinos yn rhedeg **yn g**yflym.*
	*Llinos runs **quickly**: yn + cyflym.*
Yn	*In + Treiglad Trwynol [BUT: In + language + Treiglad Meddal]*

*Dw i wedi gadael fy llyfr **yn** y car.*
*I have left my book **in** the car.*
*Dw i wedi gadael fy llyfr **yng ngh**ar fy ffrind.*
*I have left my book **in** my friend's car.*
*Mae'r llyfr **yn** Gymraeg.*
*The book is **in** Welsh.*

Yn ôl / 'Nôl   (i) Back
*Mi wnes i ddŵad **yn ôl** i Gymru i fyw.*
*I came **back** to Wales to live.*
(ii) According to
Yn ôl ein tiwtor, dan ni'n siarad yn dda!
According to our tutor, we speak well!

Yna   *There*
*Does 'na ddim byd **yna**.*
*There's nothing **there**.*

Yr Alban   Scotland
*Mae Fiona'n dŵad o Glasgow yn **yr Alban**.*
*Fiona comes from Glasgow in **Scotland**.*

Yr Eidal   Italy
*Dach chi wedi bod ym Milan yn **yr Eidal** erioed?*
*Have you ever been in Milan in **Italy**?*

Ysbyty [eg]   Hospital
> ysbytai   *Mi wnaethon ni fynd i'r **ysbyty** ar ôl y ddamwain.*
*We went to the **hospital** after the accident.*

Ysgol [eb]   School
> ysgolion   *Mi fydd fy mhlentyn yn dechrau yn yr **ysgol** y mis nesa.*
*My child will be starting in **school** next month.*

Ysgrifennu (at) *To write [to a person]:* [Also: **Sgrifennu / Sgwennu**]
*Dw i'n mynd i **ysgrifennu** llythyr.*
*I'm going to **write** a letter.*

Dw i'n mynd i **ysgrifennu** *llythyr* **at** *fy merch.*
I'm going to **write** *a letter* **to** *my daughter /*
I'm going to **write** *my daughter a letter.*

Ysgrifenedig* *Written, in writing*

Ysgrifenyddes *[eb] Secretary [female]*

> ysgrifenyddesau *Mae hi'n gweithio fel* **ysgrifenyddes** *yn yr ysgol newydd.*
She's working as a **secretary** *in the new school.*

Ysgrifennydd *[eg] Secretary [male]*

> ysgrifenyddion *Mae o'n gweithio fel* **ysgrifennydd** *yn yr ysgol newydd.*
He's working as a **secretary** *in the new school.*

Ysmygu *See >* **Smygu**

Ystafell *See >* **Stafell**

NUMBERS 1 – 100 and 1,000

1	Un Un **d**rws Un **g**adair
2	Dau / Dwy Dau **dd**rws Dwy **g**adair
3	Tri / Tair Tri **d**rws Tair **c**adair
4	Pedwar / Pedair Pedwar **d**rws Pedair **c**adair
5	Pum[p] Pum **d**rws Pum **c**adair
6	Chwe[ch] Chwe **d**rws Chwe **c**adair / Chwe **ch**adair
7	Saith Saith **d**rws Saith **c**adair
8	Wyth Wyth **d**rws Wyth **c**adair
9	Naw Naw **d**rws Naw **c**adair
10	Deg Deg **d**rws Deg **c**adair
11	Un deg un > Un ar ddeg *[when telling the time]*
	*Mae'n **un ar ddeg** o'r gloch = 11:00*
12	Un deg dau / dwy > Deuddeg *[when telling the time]*
	*Mae'n **ddeuddeg** o'r gloch = 12:00*
13	Un deg tri / tair
14	Un deg pedwar / pedair
15	Un deg pump
16	Un deg chwech
17	Un deg saith
18	Un deg wyth
19	Un deg naw
20	Dau ddeg > Ugain munud *[when telling the time]*
	*Mae'n **ugain** munud wedi wyth = 08:20*
	*Mae'n **ugain** munud i bedwar = 03:40*
21	Dau ddeg un
22	Dau ddeg dau / dwy
23	Dau ddeg tri / tair

24	Dau ddeg pedwar / pedair
25	Dau ddeg pump > Pum munud ar hugain

[when telling the time]

Mae'n **bum munud ar hugain** *wedi dau yn y prynhawn = 14:25*

Mae'n **bum munud ar hugain** *i bump yn y prynhawn = 16:35*

26	Dau ddeg chwech
27	Dau ddeg saith
28	Dau ddeg wyth
29	Dau ddeg naw
30	Tri deg
31	Tri deg un
32	Tri deg dau / dwy
33	Tri deg tri / tair
34	Tri deg pedwar / pedair
35	Tri deg pump
36	Tri deg chwech
37	Tri deg saith
38	Tri deg wyth
39	Tri deg naw
40	Pedwar deg
41	Pedwar deg un
42	Pedwar deg dau / dwy
43	Pedwar deg tri / tair
44	Pedwar deg pedwar / pedair
45	Pedwar deg pump
46	Pedwar deg chwech
47	Pedwar deg saith
48	Pedwar deg wyth
49	Pedwar deg naw
50	Pum deg
51	Pum deg un
52	Pum deg dau / dwy

53	Pum deg tri / tair
54	Pum deg pedwar / pedair
55	Pum deg pump
56	Pum deg chwech
57	Pum deg saith
58	Pum deg wyth
59	Pum deg naw
60	Chwe deg
61	Chwe deg un
62	Chwe deg dau / dwy
63	Chwe deg tri / tair
64	Chwe deg pedwar / pedair
65	Chwe deg pump
66	Chwe deg chwech
67	Chwe deg saith
68	Chwe deg wyth
69	Chwe deg naw
70	Saith deg
71	Saith deg un
72	Saith deg dau / dwy
73	Saith deg tri / tair
74	Saith deg pedwar / pedair
75	Saith deg pump
76	Saith deg chwech
77	Saith deg saith
78	Saith deg wyth
79	Saith deg naw
80	Wyth deg
81	Wyth deg un
82	Wyth deg dau / dwy
83	Wyth deg tri / tair
84	Wyth deg pedwar / pedair
85	Wyth deg pump
86	Wyth deg chwech

87	Wyth deg saith
88	Wyth deg wyth
89	Wyth deg naw
90	Naw deg
91	Naw deg un
92	Naw deg dau / dwy
93	Naw deg tri / tair
94	Naw deg pedwar / pedair
95	Naw deg pump
96	Naw deg chwech
97	Naw deg saith
98	Naw deg wyth
99	Naw deg naw
100	Cant
1,000	Mil

1af / Cynta   *1st*
Dyma'r cwestiwn **cynta** */ Dyma'r uned* **gynta**.
This is the **first** *question / This is the* **first** *unit.*

2il /Ail   *2nd + Treiglad Meddal*
Dyma'r **ail** *gwestiwn / Dyma'r* **ail** *uned.*
This is the **second** *question / This is the* **second** *unit.*

3ydd / Trydydd   *3rd + masculine nouns*
Dyma'r **trydydd** *cwestiwn.*
This is the **third** *question.*

3edd / Trydedd   *3rd + feminine nouns + Treiglad Meddal*
Dyma'r **drydedd** *uned.*
This is the **third** *unit.*

HOW TO LEARN A VOCABULARY

LANGUAGE COURSES often give the impression that you can speak a language by learning a few simple expressions and a few handfuls of words. If all you want to do is buy a cup of coffee or a bus ticket, then this is probably true. But if, like most people, you lead a life which is not entirely predictable, you will soon meet situations where you need a much bigger vocabulary than the words you have been taught in class. Everyday language in Welsh uses thousands of words, but many of these words are not used very often. This means that you need to have two main strategies to be able to cope with the Welsh you will meet outside your classroom. The first strategy is that you need to know the 2,000 or so most frequent words in Welsh, to be able to recognise them instantly, and to be able to use them fluently. Knowing these words means that you will be able to recognise about 80% of all the words you will come across on a regular basis. This is a good start, but to be a fluent performer in Welsh, 2,000 words is only the beginning. If you want to become really fluent then you need to develop a much bigger vocabulary – 10,000 words or more.

Ten thousand words is a lot, and you cannot expect your teacher to teach them to you. When you go to a Welsh class, you will perhaps learn ten new words in an hour, so in a ten-week evening class, two hours a week, you can expect to pick up about 200 new words, if you are lucky. Unfortunately, most people forget about half of the new words they learn in class, so your total vocabulary uptake from a class of this sort might be as little as a hundred new words. Obviously, we have a problem here: if you need to develop a large vocabulary, then it's not reasonable to expect to learn them all in class. There are just too many words to learn, and your teacher doesn't have the time to teach them all individually. This means that you need to develop techniques that will help you take charge of your own word learning, and build up your vocabulary outside of your Welsh classes. Successful language learners have always used these techniques, and if you are serious about learning Welsh, then you should learn how to use them too.

These notes discuss ten methods that are generally reckoned to be successful ways of learning words. You might find that the techniques don't all work for you. This is because not all learners are alike: some learners work best with written input, some learners work best with spoken input; some learners can't wait to try out new words they have learned, while others are not confident about using their language in public and prefer to work in private; some learners read a lot while others hardly ever pick up a book. Whatever kind of learner you are, some of the techniques in this article will work for you. When you find the ones that work, develop them for yourself. Remember, when it comes to learning vocabulary, the only person who can do it is you.

1 Set yourself a daily target

The first thing you need to do to take charge of your vocabulary learning is to set yourself a daily target. It doesn't really matter what this target is, though it needs to be a realistic one. For most people, it's NOT realistic to set a target of 50 words a day. On the other hand, a target of one word a day IS realistic, but isn't going to get you very far. So set yourself a target of two or three words a day: this is enough to be challenging, and if you keep it up then you will have learned nearly a thousand words in a year. The trick is to be absolutely systematic about this: do it every day, including weekends and holidays. Learning new words needs to become part of your daily routine, like brushing your teeth.

This method is particularly important for beginners. This book will provide you with some particularly important words which occur frequently in everyday Welsh.

2 Learn to use a Memory System

It's almost impossible to learn new words just by looking at lists in a book. Serious language learners use a memory system. Some people claim that they can learn hundreds of words in a few hours using these systems, but it's much better to learn a few words at a time. Memory systems are particularly useful for beginners, who can greatly benefit from developing their vocabulary at a very fast rate.

The best memory system is the linkword method. At first sight, this method looks a bit complicated, but it really does work. Here is what you have to do to use this method.

Suppose you want to learn the word *ci*, meaning *dog*. First, find an English word that sounds a bit like *ci*. A good one to use would be KEY, which sounds almost exactly like *ci*. Next, make up a picture which involves a DOG and a KEY. For example, you might think of a clockwork DOG with a large KEY sticking out of its back, or you might think of a DOG carrying a large KEY in its mouth, or a DOG burying a big KEY instead of a bone. Basically, any image that links DOG and KEY will work, but in general funny images, or bizarre ones, work best. Think about this image for a few seconds. What you are doing here is building a chain of connections between *ci* and DOG, with KEY forming a link between them, like this:

ci   KEY   dog

It's very easy to remember that *ci* and KEY go together because they both sound the same. It's also easy to remember KEY and DOG, because we have created a funny image involving a dog doing something odd with a key. This creates an almost automatic link between *ci* and *DOG*.

The reason the linkword method works is because it helps you remember the shape of the words that you are trying to learn. If you think of a word as consisting of two parts, a FORM and a MEANING, most people think that the hard part about learning words is remembering which MEANING goes with a particular FORM. In fact, the really hard thing about learning new words is remembering the FORM long enough for a MEANING to become attached to it. The linkword method makes the FORMS easier to remember. It takes a bit of extra effort, but after a while you will find that you don't need the linkword any more: you just have a direct connection between *ci* and *dog*.

It's not always easy to find keywords for Welsh words, because the shape of Welsh words is very different from the shape of English words. Your linkword doesn't have to be a complete match to the Welsh word you are trying to learn – often just a part of the word will do.

Sometimes, you can find a linkword that doesn't rely on a visual image. For example, if you are trying to learn *telyn* (meaning *harp*), then you might decide that *telyn* sounds a bit like TELL LYNNE, and you could make up a a short sentence like *Tell Lynne about the harp* to help you remember *telyn,* like this:

telyn   Tell Lynne about the harp   harp

Some people find these verbal images much more effective than visual ones. Work out which one works best for you.

3 Watch out for 'free' words

Although Welsh vocabulary looks very hard at first sight, there are actually a lot of 'free' words in Welsh that you will know already, and other 'almost free' words that are easy to recognise once your vocabulary starts to grow. Over the years, Welsh has borrowed lots of words from English, and they are very easy to recognise. Welsh has also adopted a lot of words which might be familiar to you in other languages: *ffenest* (window) is a bit like *fenêtre* in French – both of them come from the Latin word for window; *eglwys* (church) sounds a bit like French *église* – they both come from the Latin word for church *ecclesia,* which also pops up in the English word *ecclesiastical*; *ceffyl* (horse) looks a bit like the French word *cheval* – they both come from the Latin word for horse; *cadair* (chair) is related to the English word *cathedral* – a church where a bishop's *throne* is located.

Difficult-looking Welsh words are often made up from smaller easier ones, and you should try to recognise these small words in the new words you are learning. *Llyfrgell* (library) is made up of *llyfr* (book) and *cell* (store); *llawlyfr* (a manual) is made up from *llaw* (hand) and *llyfr* (book); *mewnfudiad* (immigration) is made up from *mewn* (in) and *mudiad* (movement). Welsh has lots of words like this, and it will greatly help you if you can learn to recognise them.

There are also some systematic correspondences between the beginnings of Welsh words and the beginnings of English words. Words that begin with AIL- are often related to English words that begin with RE- (*ailagor* – ail + agor = reopen; *ailfeddwl* – ail + meddwl = rethink). Words that begin with CYD- are often related to English words that start with CO- (*cydweithio* – cyd + gweithio = cooperate). Words that begin with CAM- often relate to English words beginning with MIS- (*cam-drin*

– cam + trin = mistreat; *camarwain* – cam + arwain = mislead). If you keep an eye out for correspondences of this sort, you will significantly reduce your learning load, particularly for less usual words.

4 Learn new words in context

Learning new words in a context is a lot easier than trying to learn lists of words and their meanings. A good way to do this is to use headlines from magazines. Headlines are usually quite short, and they carry a lot of information. For example, a word like *ystyried* (consider) is quite difficult to learn on its own, but in a context like: *Ystyried codi trydedd bont dros y Fenai* (Consider building a third bridge across the Menai Strait) is much easier to remember. If you buy a copy of the Welsh weekly magazine *Golwg*, then you will find lots of examples of this sort. These headlines come with the added advantage of being fairly topical, and this means that they may contain words that you are likely to meet in other contexts, such as listening to the Welsh-language news on S4C.

A good way to work with headline contexts is to find a headline that contains a word you don't know. Look up the meaning of the unknown word in a dictionary, and write the headline out on a small card. On the back of the card write the unknown word. Keep a stack of these cards somewhere handy. Then once a day work through your stack of cards. Look at the back of the card and try to recall the meaning of the word. If you don't know it, turn the card over, and the context should be enough to jog your memory. Doing this ten times should fix the word in your memory without too much extra effort.

5 Read something every day

The only reliable way to build up a very large vocabulary quickly is by reading, and you should make a point of reading something every day. Be sensible about what you choose to read. Heavy literature and serious novels are not a good idea for beginners – no one can read a story if they have to look up two or three words in each line in a dictionary. In any case, works of this kind will contain lots of words that aren't useful for you. A good thing to read is a storybook aimed at young children: the story-lines in these texts will usually be predictable and easy to understand, and there are usually lots of pictures in books of this sort, which will help you to guess the meanings of words you don't know. Storybooks for children usually have a lot of repetition in them too, and repetition increases your chances of learning new words. The more often a word appears in what you read, the more likely you are to learn it, so don't be embarrassed by reading books that seem really simple and childish. They WILL help you acquire a basic vocabulary. And don't be afraid to read the same book several times.

For beginners, audiobooks are a useful way to read. Listen to the story at the same time as you read the words on the page.

If you are able to read slightly more advanced stories, where there is more text and fewer pictures, then there is a good trick that you can do to convince yourself that your vocabulary is getting bigger. Find a story which you can just about read with the help of a dictionary. Start reading, and keep going until you have had to look up ten words, then stop. Count how many lines of text you read, and keep a record of this figure. Next day, read what you read yesterday (this will rehearse the new words you learned yesterday, and remind you of what the story is about). Then read on until you have found another ten words that you had to look up. Count the number of lines you read before you reached ten new words. You should find that you can gradually extend the number of lines you can read before you meet the ten-word threshold.

Another good idea with reading is to take a text that you know well in English and find a translation in Welsh. Then read a couple of paragraphs in English, and read the same couple of paragraphs in the Welsh translation. The fact that you already know what the Welsh text means will make it easy for you to 'understand' the Welsh, and to guess the meanings of any words that you don't know.

6 Write something every day

When you learn new words, it's a good idea to use them as soon as possible. There are two ways to do this. One is to engineer a situation where you can use the word in a natural context. For example if you learn the word for carrots (*moron*), make a point of going to buy carrots at your local friendly Welsh-speaking greengrocer's shop as soon as possible. If this isn't possible, then the best thing you can do is just write this word down in a short sentence. As with reading, it's a good idea to keep a list of 'writing words'. Write your new word on the back of a small card, and write a phrase or a short sentence that contains this word on the front. When you have a stack of these cards, you can work through them one at a time, reviewing the sentences you already wrote, and adding a new sentence on each card. By the time you have done this five or six times over the course of a few days, you should have learnt the new words.

7 Listen to songs

There is a lot of evidence that words you learn in musical contexts are much better learned than words that you only meet in speech. Some psychologists think that this is because musical input is processed deep inside your brain, whereas ordinary speech is processed in a shallower way. Either way, there is a lot of evidence that people are much more likely to remember songs than they are to remember ordinary speech, and even when you forget your first language, you are often able to remember things like nursery rhymes and chants that you knew in childhood. Songs with good lyrics often have a chorus which repeats some of the main words in the lyrics, and this provides an added support. What you need to do here is listen to the same songs over and over until you know them off by heart, and can sing along with the artist. You can start by listening and reading the lyrics, but after a while, you should find that you can manage without the written lyrics.

Some people think that you can learn vocabulary more effectively if you study word lists while you listen to instrumental music, especially if you do this just before you go to bed. New Age soft background music is supposed to be very good, but the actual evidence on the effectiveness of this method is not very strong. My own view on this idea is that what makes it work is the ritual aspect of sitting down and playing a particular piece of calming music. Sitting down in the same place, with the same music, at the same time of day creates a sort of psychological space and lets you focus on the vocabulary learning task more consciously than you would otherwise.

8 Make your vocabulary fluent

Another way to practise your vocabulary is to buy a set of
picture postcards, preferably postcards of a place you are
familiar with. Take ten of the postcards and put them in a
pile. Take each postcard, and find five things that you can
name or describe. Time how long it takes you to complete
this task for all ten postcards. You should find that the
completion time goes down steadily if you do this task once
a week. After a while, however, the completion time will
level out and stop getting shorter. When that happens you
should increase the number of words you find for each card.
When you can generate ten words for each postcard without
hesitating, stop counting the words you know really well
and find a more difficult word. For example, if your postcard
is a picture of Barry Island in summer, you might decide that
mam (mum) and *plant* (children) or *môr* (*sea*) are too easy,
and try other words instead. Alternatively, you could start
to look for two-word phrases instead of single words (*mam
hapus*, or *plant bach*). If you do this task regularly, you will
find that you start noticing new words that you could use
with your postcards, and this will make it easier for you to
learn them.

The idea here is that repeating this task will show you
how much better you are getting, and how much more fluent
your use of Welsh words is becoming.

9 Watch DVDs with subtitles

A really good way of increasing your vocabulary is to
watch DVDs and TV programmes that use subtitles.
There are two ways of doing this. One is to watch Welsh-
language programmes with English subtitles. This will
help you understand what you are listening to. Even if

you cannot catch exactly what words are being used, you will understand what is being said, and this will make it more likely that you will catch the words another time. This idea works particularly well if you can watch the same programme several times over – you can do this if you get hold of some Welsh-language films which come with English subtitles. The other way to use subtitles is to watch Welsh-language TV programmes with subtitles in Welsh provided for people who are hard of hearing. This has the advantage that you can actually see the words that are being spoken. Same language subtitles make it very much easier to catch what is being said, and will help you recognise new words more quickly. If you have a CD-ROM with Welsh-language subtitles, then you can try turning the sound down and reading the subtitles out loud. You have to be pretty quick to do this, as the subtitles remain on screen for a fairly short time. Again, this works best if you watch a film that you are already familiar with. Keep track of how many subtitles you can read out loud before they disappear. You should find that the number goes up each time you do this task.

10 Use your local resources

In most localities in Wales there is lots of Welsh on the street. Make sure that you can read and understand any notices in your area. Make sure that you can translate your local street names. If you live in a strongly Welsh-speaking area you will find that lots of houses where you live will have Welsh names – make sure that you understand all the ones in the streets near you.

The ten techniques that I have outlined here will provide you with a set of simple tools for picking up new words and making them part of your own vocabulary. The key message here is **do it yourself!** Your teacher will only be able to teach you a few words in class, and you need to take charge of your own learning if you want to become really proficient in Welsh. It's particularly important to build up a large vocabulary incrementally, learning a few words every day over a very long time.

The ten techniques I have outlined above are all standard ideas with a lot of research to back them up. However, there is another method which I have found useful that you might be able to use for yourself. I call it the Fahrenheit 451 method, after Ray Bradbury's novel of the same name. In Bradbury's novel, society has decided that books are a bad thing, and crews of firemen track down illicit collections of books and burn them. A few people on the edge of society have decided that they must preserve these books, and they each undertake to learn a book off by heart, so that they can pass it on even when the physical texts have been destroyed. The Fahrenheit 451 method uses the same idea. It suggests that a good way to learn a very large advanced vocabulary in a foreign language is to learn a long text off by heart.

This idea is not a new one, of course. It was used a lot by nineteenth-century missionaries who would often learn new languages by memorising large parts of the Bible in the language of the country they were working in. The fact that they were very highly motivated, and the fact that they were already familiar with the English texts made it fairly simple to learn very long foreign language texts in this way, and provided the missionaries with a large vocabulary which was highly relevant to their work. The Gospel of St Mark, for example, the shortest of the four Gospels, and very familiar to any missionary, contains about 13,000 running words. If you learned that text off by heart – or even fairly well – then you would end up with a vocabulary of around 5,000 different words, and have no trouble learning what they mean and how to use them.

Learning texts off by heart is not a method that curries much favour in modern language teaching methods, but I think it might be due for a re-evaluation. The problem is that we don't have any modern texts that act as a shared reference point, as the Bible did in the nineteenth century, or the Communist Manifesto did in the twentieth century. However, if you can find a Welsh translation of a book that is particularly important to you, then give this method a try. Even a short book – one that you could read comfortably in a couple of hours – will give you a vocabulary of several thousand words.

Paul Meara

July 2014